Real Talk 1
Authentic English in Context

Teacher's Manual
with Answer Key
and Tests

Lida Baker
Judith Tanka

PEARSON
Longman

Real Talk 1
Teacher's Manual with Answer Key and Tests

Pearson Education, 10 Bank Street, White Plains, NY 10606

Staff credits: The people who made up the **Real Talk 1 Teacher's Manual with Answer Key and Tests** team, representing editorial, production, design, and manufacturing, are Elizabeth Carlson, Christine Edmonds, Nancy Flaggman, Jane Townsend, Paula Van Ells, and Patricia Wosczyk.

Text composition: Laserwords
Text font: 11/13 Times

ISBN: 0-13-1945548

Printed in the United States of America
5 6 7 8 9 10—OPM—10 09

LONGMAN ON THE **WEB**

Longman.com offers online resources for teachers and students. Access our Companion Websites, our online catalog, and our local offices around the world.

Visit us at **longman.com.**

CONTENTS

INTRODUCTION TO *REAL TALK 1*

LEVEL AND AUDIENCE

Real Talk 1 is a textbook for English language learners that uses authentic listening passages in a variety of genuine contexts as the basis for the development of listening and speaking skills. The text is designed for students at the high intermediate level in both second- and foreign-language environments. (This Teacher's Manual includes explanatory notes for the benefit of teachers located both inside and outside the United States.)

A companion text, *Real Talk 2*, is aimed at the advanced level.

AUDIO

The audio material for this book consists of recordings of "real" people (not actors) speaking naturally in four real-world contexts: in person, on the phone, on the air, and in class. The recordings include features such as false starts, fillers, hesitations, repetitions, and errors, all of which are an integral part of authentic speech. By means of carefully structured and sequenced exercises, the book teaches students how to recognize the essential information in the messy stream of sound they encounter in the real English-speaking world.

CHAPTER CONTENT AND ORGANIZATION

Real Talk 1 consists of eight chapters, each of which is organized around a general theme such as travel or shopping. Each chapter is then divided into four parts, corresponding to—and named after—the four contexts in which spoken English normally occurs, that is, In Person, On the Phone, On the Air, and In Class. The following is a brief description of the recordings in each part:

In Person: The recordings consist of face-to-face conversations, surveys, or interviews.

On the Phone: Students hear phone conversations, for example, a person calling a dating service, as well as authentic recorded announcements, such as the recorded "menu" at a ticket office.

On the Air: The recordings for this section are excerpted from a variety of radio programs and include both news and feature segments.

In Class: In this section students hear mini-lectures, typically four to six minutes in length, and learn how to take notes.

Each part above is divided into prelistening, listening, and post-listening sections. The vocabulary, teaching points, and speaking activities are drawn from the content of the listening. For a detailed description of the exercises and activities within each section, with suggestions for teaching them, see the General Teaching Tips.

SPEAKING ACTIVITIES

All three sections (prelistening, listening, post-listening) of each chapter part include speaking activities. Most skill-building activities are done in pairs or small groups, and students normally go over answers to exercises with their classmates. The post-listening section, called Real Talk: Use What You've Learned, includes a vocabulary review and communicative activities such as discussions, role plays, interviews, and debates. For more detailed information about the speaking activities, see the General Teaching Tips.

TEACHING SEQUENCE AND TIME MANAGEMENT

The pronunciation, vocabulary, and note-taking skills presented in *Real Talk 1* loosely build on one another from part to part and from chapter to chapter, especially in the first three chapters. (See the Scope and Sequence in the front of the Student Book for details.) We recommend teaching at least the early chapters in sequence. Nevertheless, it is possible to skip chapters or parts of chapters in order to accommodate the interests and needs of students. The book also lends itself to some independent study. For example, if you have some students who will be attending an English-speaking university and others who will not, you could assign Part Four: In Class to the university-bound students to do in the listening lab.

Every class is different, so it is not possible for us to state precisely how much time you will need in order to cover each chapter of *Real Talk 1*. In our field testing of the materials, Parts One to Three required between one and two hours of class time each to complete. Part Four required between two and three hours. You can reduce the class time needed by assigning some activities, such as the vocabulary work in the pre- and post-listening sections, for homework.

We hope that you and your students will find *Real Talk 1* stimulating, challenging, and easy to use.

L. B. and J. T.

Parts One to Three

Parts One to Three (In Person, On the Phone, and On the Air) have similar organization and components, which are described in this section. (Part Four: In Class is somewhat different and is described separately in the section that follows.)

A. PRELISTENING

Each chapter part opens with a prelistening section consisting of three items:

* Art
* A speaking activity
* A preview of important vocabulary from the listening

Keeping in mind that students will probably be eager to get to the listening, we advise spending no more than 20 or 30 minutes on prelistening work.

Art

Visuals consist of items related to the content of the listening, such as photographs, drawings, graphs, or newspaper headlines. The purpose of the art is to tap into students' existing knowledge and to stimulate their curiosity regarding the upcoming listening.

SUGGESTED PROCEDURE

Begin the lesson by having students look at the art. Ask questions such as the following:

* What do you see?
* How does this (photo, graph, etc.) relate to your previous experience?
* How does it make you feel?
* Based on the art, what do you think the listening will be about?

Speaking Activity

This activity, like the art, is designed to call up students' prior knowledge of the listening topic and to motivate them to listen. Most often the activity consists of a discussion, but there are also quizzes and surveys in some chapters. The directions always state the general topic of the listening to come and specify how students should be grouped.

SUGGESTED PROCEDURE

1. Read, or have a student read, the directions. Group students as directed. Announce a time limit for the activity.
2. Circulate while students are working. Answer questions and provide help as needed.
3. When time is up, bring the class back together and wrap up the activity. For example, you can summarize answers that seemed to recur from group to group, mention one or two unusual comments you heard, or correct errors. You can also ask one student from each group to summarize that group's discussion.

Vocabulary Preview

In this exercise students read sentences containing key vocabulary from the listening and match the expressions with their definitions. Sufficient context is provided so that students can do the exercise without using a dictionary. Exercise items include words and phrases that students will need in order to understand the main idea of the listening. Slang or colloquial expressions are identified with the label *informal*. You may want to read the target items out loud so that students will recognize them when they hear them in the recording.

SUGGESTED PROCEDURE
1. Read, or call on a student to read, the directions.
2. Students can work alone, in pairs, or in small groups.
3. Announce a time limit for the activity.
4. Do not allow students to use dictionaries. Encourage them to use the context to figure out the meanings. Remind students that idiomatic expressions cannot be translated word for word.
5. When time is up, go over the answers. You or a student can write them on the board, or you can go over them orally.

OPTIONAL PROCEDURE
Some teachers assign the vocabulary preview as homework to be completed before doing the listening work (see Listening below). This is one way to save time in class.

B. LISTENING

There are three activities in this section, arranged from general to specific.

Main Ideas

Here students listen to the entire recording once and answer questions targeting the main ideas of the listening. Question types include multiple choice, fill in, true/false, and open-ended questions that students answer in note form. Reassure students that they don't need to understand every word in order to comprehend the main ideas. They will be well prepared for listening if they have done the prelistening speaking and vocabulary activities.

SUGGESTED PROCEDURE
1. Read, or have a student read, the directions.
2. Instruct students to read the questions before listening. This will help them to focus their listening. Encourage them to predict the answers on the basis of the prelistening activities they have already done.
3. Play the recording. Students may answer questions while listening, but give them time afterward to finish.
4. Play the recording again if necessary.
5. Do not allow students to read the script while they are listening. Otherwise, they will be reading, not listening!
6. After listening, have students work in pairs and compare their answers to the questions.
7. Go over the answers with the whole class.

Details and Inferences

Some of the questions in this section target details from the listening. Other questions require students to draw inferences from the information in the listening.

SUGGESTED PROCEDURE

1. Go over the directions in the manner described previously.
2. Give students time to read the questions before listening. If they know the answers from their earlier listening, they may answer the questions now and check their answers when they listen again.
3. Play the recording. As in the Main Ideas section, students may begin answering questions as they listen, but give them time afterward to finish.
4. Put students in pairs and have them compare and discuss their answers.
5. Go over the answers with the whole class.
6. A useful strategy to employ when going over inference questions is to ask students, "How do you know?" This question requires them to explain which pieces of information led them to the answer they chose. In this way you can check that they did not get the correct answer by chance.
7. If you discover that students are unable to answer a question, replay the section of the recording containing the information they need. Stop the recording at that point and ask students to repeat what they heard. Ask additional questions to help students understand, but do not allow them to read the script except as a last resort. (See Using the Audioscript, page 13.)

Listening for Language

This section targets specific features of spoken English and presents explanations and exercises in a bottom-up fashion. Two kinds of activities are presented. (Most chapter parts include both types; a few contain one or the other.) The first, Focus on Sound, targets phonological features such as stress and reductions, and the second, Conversation Tools, deals with functions such as giving advice or warnings. The teaching points in these activities were selected on the basis of their occurrence and prominence in the listening.

FOCUS ON SOUND

This section begins with an explanation of a phonological feature, e.g., reductions, followed by a focused listening exercise. Some exercise items are extracted directly from the recording. Others have been written and recorded for the specific instructional purpose of the exercise. Listening is normally followed by controlled speaking practice with the targeted pronunciation feature.

SUGGESTED PROCEDURE

1. Read or have students read the explanation of the pronunciation feature.
2. Model the examples in the explanation. Check to make sure students have understood the explanation and the terminology used, e.g., *vowel, consonant, syllable.*
3. Play the recording and have students complete the task. If the task calls for students to repeat after the speaker, check to ensure that all students participate and that shy students don't remain silent. If pauses between items appear inadequate, lengthen the pause by using the hold button on your audio equipment.

4. Have students work in pairs and compare their answers.
5. Go over the answers with the whole class if necessary.

CONVERSATION TOOLS

This section begins with a list of functions (conversational phrases and idioms used for specific communicative tasks, such as apologizing or asking for clarification) and an explanation of their proper use and cultural context. The list is followed by a focused listening and/or speaking activity in which students practice the conversation tools.

SUGGESTED PROCEDURE

1. Read or have students read the list of functions. Model the correct pronunciation and explain unfamiliar vocabulary if necessary. Note that many functions are idiomatic expressions and therefore cannot be translated word for word. For example, the expression "That's a shame" has a very different meaning from the dictionary definition of the word *shame*.
2. Have students complete the listening or speaking task that follows. Monitor pairs or groups to ensure they are using the language properly.

C. REAL TALK: USE WHAT YOU'VE LEARNED

This section includes a Vocabulary Review and one or more communicative speaking activities that incorporate the skills and language presented in the previous two sections. The speaking activities include discussions, role plays, community surveys, debates, and oral presentations.

Vocabulary Review

This section reviews the words and expressions taught in the chapter part. It also includes one or more activities that elicit the unit vocabulary and allow students to think about and personalize the chapter content. Very often the Vocabulary Review is combined with a discussion (see Discussions on the next page).

You may notice that the list of words appearing in the Vocabulary Review is shorter than the list in the Vocabulary Preview activity. This is because the two lists serve different purposes: Words in the Vocabulary Preview are those which students will need in order to comprehend the main idea of the listening. The list may include low-frequency words that happen to be important in this instance. In contrast, the Vocabulary Review includes mainly high-frequency words that students should work on adding to their active vocabulary.

SUGGESTED PROCEDURE

1. Read or have students read the directions. Have them form pairs or groups as indicated.
2. *Optional step:* Have students review the meanings of the items. They can try to do this from memory. If they don't remember, they can look back at the Vocabulary Preview. Another optional step is to have students read the script, find the items, and focus on the way the items are used in context.

3. Encourage students to use the review items actively as they speak. Walk around and monitor groups to make sure they do so. Note any recurring errors in the use of the target vocabulary. Also take note of correct, innovative uses of the new words and phrases.
4. Bring the class back together. Go over the errors you noted. Also share correct uses of the new vocabulary and praise students for their effort. Finally, have students share interesting, surprising, or controversial answers that emerged during the review activity.

OPTIONAL HOMEWORK
For additional practice with the new vocabulary, assign one of the following tasks:

* Have students write their own sentences using the new vocabulary. This can be done on paper or in a vocabulary notebook, which students turn in periodically for you to check.
* Have students write a composition related to the theme of the chapter part. Encourage them to use as much of the new vocabulary as possible.
* Have students use a search engine or an online concordance and record examples of authentic uses of the vocabulary. (For help, see the article "The Compleat Lexical Tutor" in the TESL Electronic Journal, http://www-writing.berkeley.edu/TESL-EJ/.)

Discussions

Nearly every part of every chapter includes a discussion activity in which students are able to share their own experiences and opinions about the topic of the lesson. Often the Vocabulary Review is coupled with a discussion so that students can use the new vocabulary while discussing questions related to the content of the recording.

SUGGESTED PROCEDURE
1. Read the directions and place students in pairs or groups.
2. If questions are provided, have students take turns reading the questions out loud.
3. Emphasize that everyone needs to participate in the discussion. If necessary, review expressions for interrupting, asking for repetition, and keeping the conversation going.
4. As students are talking, circulate and monitor the discussion. Answer questions and take notes on items you want to go over when the discussion is finished.
5. Leave a few minutes at the end to bring the class back together and wrap up the discussion. Use this time to make comments, go over errors, and get feedback from students on their conversation.

Role Plays

This type of activity presents students with scenarios in which they assume roles and act out situations in pairs, in groups, or in front of the whole class.

SUGGESTED PROCEDURE
1. When possible, bring in props or costumes to add drama and fun to the role play.
2. As always, begin by reading the directions. Follow the directions for grouping students and assigning roles.

3. If students are not familiar with role playing, act out a sample with an outgoing student volunteer.
4. Give students plenty of time to plan their role play and rehearse.
5. While students are preparing, circulate, answer questions, and offer suggestions.
6. If students perform their role plays in front of the whole class, begin by calling for volunteers.
7. If your class is large, students can perform their role plays for one or two other pairs or groups.

OPTIONAL PROCEDURES

1. If you plan to have students perform their role plays in front of the class, have one pair practice with another pair before doing it in front of the whole group.
2. If students are very shy or inexperienced or lack fluency, have them write a script to use while they are rehearsing. When they perform in front of the class, encourage them to do so without the script but allow them to use it if they are very nervous or fearful.
3. Another option for fearful students is to have them write key words on a note card.
4. An option for highly fluent and outgoing students is to perform their role play extemporaneously, i.e., with no time to rehearse.
5. Once students are very familiar and comfortable with role playing, record or videotape their role plays and have them listen to or view themselves "in action."

INTERVIEWS AND SURVEYS

In these speaking activities students gather information from each other or, if possible, from English speakers outside their class, using a set of questions provided in the text or written by the students themselves. For surveys in which students talk with more than one person, a chart is usually provided in which they can take notes on the answers they collect.

Some activities ask students to interview English speakers. If that is not possible, do one of the following:

* Have students interview you and/or other English-speaking teachers at your school.
* Have them interview people they know who do not speak English, but instruct students to record the answers they collect in English and to report on the answers in class in English.

SUGGESTED PROCEDURE

Follow the detailed instructions in the Student Book for grouping students, preparing the questions, carrying out the interview or survey (in class or out), and following up with the whole class.

OPTIONAL PROCEDURE

As a follow-up, have students write compositions about the questions they asked, the answers they collected, and their opinion or interpretation of the responses they heard.

INFORMATION GAPS

In these activities, students in pairs or groups are given different or partial sets of information. This creates a "gap" in the knowledge that different participants have, and they must speak to one another in order to piece together a complete set of information. For example, students may work together to solve a puzzle, fill in a chart, put things in the right order, or find similarities and differences between pictures.

SUGGESTED PROCEDURE

1. Follow the instructions in the Student Book for grouping students and carrying out the activity. The information for Student A will usually be found on the same page as the instructions for the activity. The information for Student B (and occasionally Student C) will be found at the end of the chapter.

2. Remind students not to show each other their information.

3. Once students have read their own information, it will be time to begin talking and sharing. This will usually involve using the phonological features and conversation tools taught in that part of the chapter. Circulate, provide help as needed, and monitor students' language use. Note significant errors.

4. When students finish, each person should have a complete set of data. Partners or group members should look at one another's papers to make sure they got everything right.

5. Bring the class back together and discuss any interesting or unusual facts that emerged from the activity.

Part Four

In this part of the chapter students hear an academic mini-lecture and learn how to take notes. At the beginning of the course, take a few moments to explain why note-taking is important. Students who plan to study at a North American university will need to use their lecture notes whenever they study for a test because exams include information from both lectures and books. Non-academic students also benefit from note-taking because the process of listening and taking notes requires students to think in English, which in turn helps them to develop their fluency in the language.

A. PRELISTENING

This section consists of activities similar to those in Parts One to Three. Students are asked to respond to a visual prompt (photo, graph, drawing), discuss their background knowledge about the topic, and complete a vocabulary preview exercise. The purpose of these activities is to elicit interest in the lecture topic, to allow students to share what they already know about it, and to provide essential language that they will need in order to comprehend the content of the lecture. For additional instructions, see the recommended procedures under Prelistening, page 3.

B. LISTENING AND NOTE-TAKING

This section begins with a presentation of one or more academic note-taking skills, determined by the particular organization and language of the lecture. This focused skill work prepares students for

- the organizational pattern of the lecture they will hear (cause-effect, pro-con, etc.);
- the language (specific expressions) that provides cues to the speaker's organization;
- the form of the lecture notes that students need to take—generally an outline.

The items above are taught in sections called Lecture Form, Lecture Language, and Lecture Organization, respectively. Chapter 1 has all three sections. Subsequent chapters have two out of the three.

Lecture Organization

This section begins with a description of the organizational structure or pattern the students need to recognize in the lecture. For example, there are explanations of why introductions are important, how lecturers present the pro and con sides of an issue, or how speakers move from one topic to the next. The explanation is then followed by a listening task that provides focused practice with this teaching point.

SUGGESTED PROCEDURE

1. Read or have students read the explanation. Give them ample time to absorb the information, ask questions, and understand the examples given.
2. Read the directions to the listening task and make sure students understand what to do.
3. Play the recording and monitor students as they complete the task. Some exercises may require that you pause the recording between items. Depending on your students' level of comprehension, you may want to extend the pauses or replay some items if necessary.
4. It is often helpful to stop the recording after students have done the first item and check that they are doing the task correctly.
5. After listening, have students share and compare their answers in pairs. Encourage them to discuss the reasons for their answers.

Lecture Form

Here students learn the basics of efficient note-taking, such as using abbreviations and symbols and organizing information on a page to show what is a main point, a detail, an example, etc. A list of commonly used symbols and abbreviations is included in Appendix 2 of the Student Book, but you should encourage students to develop their own system of "telegraphic" writing. In addition, feel free to allow students to take notes in ways other than the traditional outline form. Some other ways of arranging notes on a page may include using columns, boxes, or some other visual representation of relationships between ideas. (Some of these alternative ways of note-taking are introduced in *Real Talk 2*.) The goal is for students to be able to note important information in a clear and comprehensible way that will enable them to recall key points.

SUGGESTED PROCEDURE
Follow the recommended procedures described under Lecture Organization above.

Lecture Language

This section teaches commonly used words and phrases that signal relationships between ideas or provide clues to the organization of the lecture. Understanding and recognizing these phrases will greatly enhance students' ability to predict and comprehend the content.

The teaching material consists of an explanation and a list of words and phrases, followed by a listening exercise based on one or more excerpts from the lecture. Students must recognize and/or use the words and phrases from the list in order to complete the task.

SUGGESTED PROCEDURE
Follow the recommended procedures described under Lecture Organization, page 10.

Taking Notes

In this activity students hear the entire lecture and practice the note-taking skills they have learned. In the real world, students normally take notes on their own paper. Following the lecture they may reorganize and copy their notes. We recommend the same procedure for this activity. That is, students should take notes on their own paper, then edit and rewrite their notes by filling in the incomplete outline provided in the Student Book. We do not recommend listening and taking notes directly in the book.

SUGGESTED PROCEDURES
1. Read or call on a student to read the directions. Before listening, have students look at the incomplete outline and the margin notes. Also have students examine any visuals that accompany the lecture. Tell them to pay special attention to
   * The overall form and organization of the lecture
   * What information is already in the outline
   * What key points to listen for as indicated in the margin notes
2. Encourage students to make predictions about what they will hear.
3. Remind students:
   * To use note-taking skills taught previously, such as indenting, abbreviating, and not writing complete sentences
   * To aim for understanding the key points rather than 100 percent of the lecture
   * Not to panic if they miss a major point, but instead to leave space in their notes because speakers often recycle information or summarize it in the conclusion
4. Have students close their books. Play the recording and have students take notes on their own paper.
5. In the early chapters it may be quite hard for students to listen and take notes at the same time. Model the process by playing the recording and writing notes on the board or an overhead projector transparency while students watch.
6. Replay sections that are difficult for the class.
7. After listening, have students edit and rewrite their notes using the outline in their book. *Note:* As students work through the chapters and become more comfortable with note-taking, the amount of scaffolding is gradually reduced.

If students are having difficulty taking notes, especially in the early chapters of the book, the following techniques may be helpful:

- Allow students to listen to the entire lecture the first time without taking any notes.
- Allow them to listen while looking at the outline in the book, but do not have them take notes until the second listening.
- While students are listening to the lecture, pause the recording at regular intervals to give them time to catch up, ask questions, or make predictions about what is coming next.
- Divide the class into groups and have each group take notes on just one part of the lecture. Afterward, have students share and combine their notes as they rewrite them in their books.

If you have students whose listening skill is significantly below that of the rest of the class, you can allow them either to read the lecture script ahead of time or to read the script during the first listening. Then the students can listen again and take notes. Conversely, have more advanced students listen and take notes on their own paper directly after completing the prelistening work.

Reviewing the Lecture

The purpose of this section is

- To allow students to compare their notes with their classmates' and fill in information they may have missed
- To check their comprehension by discussing and reacting to the lecture content

SUGGESTED PROCEDURE

1. Read the directions and group students as directed.
2. Have students respond to the questions orally by referring to their notes. If key information is missing, they will not be able to answer and will need to consult their classmates. Monitor groups or pairs and note whether a large number of students missed the same information. If so, you may want to do one or more of the following:
   - Provide the missing information to the whole class
   - Replay the segment of the lecture that contains the information they missed
   - Discuss with the class possible reasons why they missed the information the first time (unfamiliar vocabulary, speed of delivery, the complexity or unfamiliarity of the topic)
3. Refer students to Appendix 3 in the Student Book so that they may compare their notes to a "perfect" model. (But remind students that nobody's notes are perfect in the real world! The outlines were constructed based on *written* transcripts of the lectures. Even a native speaker would not have been able to take such perfect notes while listening.)
4. During the discussion portion of this follow-up activity, encourage students to share their personal perspectives about the lecture topic. Although some of the questions ask this directly, feel free to add more prompts, such as:
   - Did you learn anything new or surprising from this lecture?
   - Do you agree with the lecturer's point of view? Which side of the issue presented here do you agree with?
   - What personal experience have you had with this subject?

C. REAL TALK: USE WHAT YOU'VE LEARNED

This section contains activities similar to those in Parts One to Three: a Vocabulary Review and one or more communicative speaking activities that incorporate the skills and language presented in the previous two sections. The speaking activities include discussions, role plays, community surveys, debates, problem-solving tasks, and oral presentations.
For more specific instructions, see the recommended procedures under Real Talk: Use What You've Learned, page 6.

Using the Audioscript

In this Teacher's Manual we have already advised you strongly not to allow students to read the audioscript while they are listening. If you allow students to do this, you have undermined their motivation to listen, and their listening skills will not improve. There is one exception to this advice: Students whose listening ability lags far behind that of their classmates may be given the script to read *before* listening. Even these students, however, should be discouraged from listening and reading at the same time. Nevertheless, the audioscript can be a useful tool in several ways.

TIPS FOR USING THE AUDIOSCRIPT

1. We recommend that you listen to the recordings and read the audioscript before the lesson. This will help you to
   - become familiar with the context that students will be working with;
   - anticipate areas that may be difficult for students.
   Non-native English-speaking teachers, who themselves may not have regular exposure to authentic spoken English, may benefit most from this preparatory step.
2. Once students have completed the listening work in a chapter part to the best of their ability, you may choose to allow them to read the audioscript and listen along. This gives many students—and teachers—a sense of "completion" at the end of a lesson.
3. Motivated students who wish to do more vocabulary work than is offered in the book may select additional items from the audioscript to learn.

Homework

Many of the prelistening and Real Talk: Use What You've Learned (post-listening) activities can be done outside of class. For example, we have suggested that the prelistening vocabulary exercise could be done at home prior to the listening lesson in order to save time in class. The following activities can also be done outside of class:

- Some of the Vocabulary Review exercises could be converted from interactive speaking activities to writing activities that students do on their own.
- In Part Four, the activity called Reviewing the Lecture could be assigned to groups of students or to individuals to do as homework.
- Most, if not all, surveys and interviews can be done outside of class.

The activities in the Listening section could be done independently in a listening lab, particularly if a student was absent and needs to make up the work. Nevertheless, because *Real Talk 1* is so highly interactive, we recommend covering as much of the material in class as possible.

Testing

This Teacher's Manual includes eight chapter tests, one for each chapter in **Real Talk 1**. The tests cover the chapter vocabulary, Conversation Tools, Focus on Sound, and Lecture Language segments.

CHAPTER TEACHING SUGGESTIONS

and

ANSWER KEY

Part One: In Person

Background

The United States comprises many different cultures, so it is difficult to generalize about the ways that people get their names. In most cases family names are passed down from generation to generation through the father. Women most often adopt their husband's names when they get married. First names can come from many sources. For example, some people name children after a relative, either living or dead. Others choose names that sound good to them or that have a special meaning. Nicknames also come from many sources. Often they are shortened forms of the person's first or last name, or they're derived from a special characteristic, skill, or mannerism that the person has.

Art

1. Name dictionaries like the one shown here are very popular in North America. There are also numerous websites dealing with baby names.
2. See the General Teaching Tips, page 3, for suggestions on presenting art.

A. PRELISTENING (page 1)

Discussion

1. See the General Teaching Tips, page 3, for suggestions on conducting prelistening speaking activities.
2. Model a response to the question by talking about your own name or the names of your family members.
3. If there are students from different countries in your class, you can conclude this activity by asking one person from each nationality to briefly answer the discussion question.

Vocabulary Preview

See the General Teaching Tips, page 4, for suggestions on conducting the vocabulary preview.

ANSWERS

1. c	**3.** e	**5.** g	**7.** a
2. d	**4.** f	**6.** b	

B. LISTENING (page 3)

Main Ideas

See the General Teaching Tips, page 4, for suggestions on teaching the Main Ideas section.

🚸 ANSWERS

1. Alia	**3.** Alia	**5.** Benjamin
2. Benjamin	**4.** Benjamin	

Details and Inferences

See the General Teaching Tips, page 5, for suggestions on teaching this section.

❸ ANSWERS

1. b	**3.** c	**5.** b	**7.** c
2. c	**4.** a	**6.** b	**8.** c

Listening for Language

See the General Teaching Tips, page 5, for suggestions on teaching this section.

FOCUS ON SOUND

1. See the General Teaching Tips, page 5, for suggestions on teaching Focus on Sound.
2. "Content" words are those which convey the essential meaning of a sentence, whereas "function" words tend to express the relationships among the content words. An utterance consisting only of content words would be understood, though perhaps not perfectly; but an utterance made up only of function words would be meaningless.
3. It may require a lot of ear training before students learn to hear the variations in pitch, volume, and intonation that characterize stressed words. This lesson is only an introduction. Point out to students that listening for stressed words is one of the most useful and most crucial strategies they must develop in order to understand spoken English. Refer back to this point frequently.
4. Students may ask you if there are additional "rules" for knowing which words to stress. Your answer should be that there are guidelines, such as the one they learned in this lesson, but not strict rules. Students should understand that a speaker can stress any word that he or she chooses to emphasize. Besides, there are great variations in the way individuals speak. However, the most basic lesson students need to learn about stress is that English speakers stress information-carrying words. Knowing this can help students get the main idea of an utterance.

EXPANSION ACTIVITIES TO TRAIN STUDENTS TO HEAR STRESSED WORDS

* Take any audio passage, transcribe it, and replace the stressed words with blanks that students fill in as they listen. This helps students to both see and hear where the stressed words are.
* Dictate sentences and have students write only the stressed words. Then have them reconstruct the full sentences using the stressed words as cues.
* Again take any audio passage and transcribe it. Underline selected words in each sentence, some stressed and some unstressed. Play the audio for students sentence by sentence. Have them tell you whether each underlined word is stressed or not.

❺ ANSWERS

1. brother	5. sense	9. English	13. Bible
2. minutes	6. last	10. Jonah	14. know
3. months	7. that	11. swallowed	15. story
4. that	8. common	12. whale	

1. See the General Teaching Tips, page 6, for suggestions on teaching Conversation Tools.
2. In Exercise 8, have students form the following questions to ask their partner about the origin or reason for their name:
   - What is the origin of your name?
   - Where did your name come from?
   - Who are you named after (for)?
   - Why did your parents give you this name?
3. For Exercise 9, provide a model if you see that students aren't sure what to do, for example: "I interviewed Stella. Her full name is Stella Maura Finel. The name Stella came from her father's mother, who was born in Italy. Stella means "star" in Latin. Maura means "dark" in Latin. She got this name because her mother liked the sound of it. And Finel, her last name, comes from her father's family. It is a very unusual name, and she doesn't know what it means."

C. REAL TALK: USE WHAT YOU'VE LEARNED (page 7)

Vocabulary Review: Discussion

1. See the General Teaching Tips, page 6, for suggestions on conducting the vocabulary review.
2. Be sure to circulate as students are talking. Note cases where students use the vocabulary being reviewed both correctly and incorrectly.
3. The discussion may not generate all the words in the list. In case you don't hear any examples of some items (such as *medieval*), ask students to make sentences with those words during the wrap-up phase of the activity.

Role Play

1. See the General Teaching Tips, page 7, for suggestions on conducting role plays.
2. More examples of real celebrity names include:

Prince: Prince Rogers Nelson
Ringo Starr: Richard Starkey
Charlie Sheen: Carlos Irwin Estevez
Demi Moore: Demetria Gene Guynes
Madonna: Madonna Louise Ciccone
Elvis Costello: Declan Patrick McManus
Tom Cruise: Thomas Cruise Mapother IV
Coolio: Artis Ivey Jr.
Eminem: Marshall Bruce Mathers III
Queen Latifah: Dana Owens
Sting: Gordon Matthew Sumner

INTERVIEW AN ENGLISH SPEAKER

We have included exercises like this throughout the book although we know that many students rarely or never have the opportunity to meet native speakers of English. Perhaps your students, working as a group, could interview you or another teacher who speaks English well. You could also pretend to be someone else—a real or imaginary character—and have the class interview your character. If that is not feasible, then you will probably have to skip this activity.

Part Two: On the Phone

Background

In this part students will hear two women talking about the decision by one of them to change her name legally. In the United States it is possible to do this by filling out paperwork and then going before a judge. (Women who marry and take their husband's name do not have to do this.) Changing one's name is not a common thing to do, but it is not rare either.

Art

See the General Teaching Tips, page 3, for suggestions on presenting art.

A. PRELISTENING (page 8)

Discussion

1. See the General Teaching Tips, page 3, for suggestions on conducting prelistening speaking activities.
2. If you are teaching in a country where changing one's name is impossible, such that students have never heard of anyone doing this, tell students the information in the background note above, but do not tell them the specific topic of the listening activity.

Vocabulary Preview

See the General Teaching Tips, page 4, for suggestions on conducting the vocabulary preview.

ANSWERS

1. d	**3.** g	**5.** h	**7.** b
2. e	**4.** f	**6.** c	**8.** a

B. LISTENING (page 9)

Main Ideas

See the General Teaching Tips, page 4, for suggestions on teaching the Main Ideas section.

ANSWERS
1. She wants to ask Judy something. / She wants to ask Judy how she changed her name legally.
2. changing her last name
3. She can't stand it. It's too long, and people often mispronounce it.
4. downtown at the courthouse

Details and Inferences

See the General Teaching Tips, page 5, for suggestions on teaching this section.

② ANSWERS

1. T
2. F (Judy was divorced in the past.)
3. F (Judy says it probably didn't cost much.)
4. F (She says it was a hassle.)

5. T
6. T
7. F (It's not definite. She says she has to decide if she's really going to go through with it.)

Listening for Language

See the General Teaching Tips, page 5, for suggestions on teaching this section.

FOCUS ON SOUND

1. See the General Teaching Tips, page 5, for suggestions on teaching Focus on Sound.
2. Be sure to model the example sentences, but don't exaggerate the stress on the negative words. While negative words are stressed in normal speech, so are the verbs that follow them. The negatives would receive exaggerated stress only if the speaker were correcting or contradicting something that had been said previously, for example:

   A: Jay is rolling in money.
   B: What are you talking about? Jay doesn't have ANY money.

④ ANSWERS

1. don't remember, cost
2. Probably, not, much
3. don't laugh, OK, really, can't stand, last name
4. You, never told, that
5. not ready, tell anybody
6. Sure, no problem, Great, talk, soon, Reka

CONVERSATION TOOLS

1. See the General Teaching Tips, page 6, for suggestions on teaching Conversation Tools.
2. The most common fillers in American English are "um," "uh," "you know," "well." Other varieties of English have different fillers. For example, many British English speakers say "em" instead of "um."

⑥ SAMPLE CONVERSATION

Reka: Hello. I'm calling to find out about name changes. Uh, what do I need to do, I mean, where can I get a legal name change?

Clerk: Well, first you have to come down to the courthouse. Um, do you know where that is?

Reka: I'm not sure.

Clerk: The address is 111 Hill Street, OK? That's on the corner of Hill and First streets.

Reka: OK, I got it. And, um, can you tell me which forms I need to fill out?

Clerk: There's a whole name-change packet you can pick up in room 112.

Reka: Oh, OK, I see. Uh, how much does it cost?

Clerk: There's a filing fee of . . . let me see . . . $94.00.

Reka: All right. And one more question, um, can you tell me how long it takes?

Clerk: Six to eight weeks.

C. REAL TALK: USE WHAT YOU'VE LEARNED (page 12)

Vocabulary Review: Describing Pictures

See the General Teaching Tips, page 6, for suggestions on conducting the vocabulary review.

POSSIBLE ANSWERS

    A. Woman catching taxi: "I've got to run."

    B. Student filling out applications: "Look at this bunch of applications. What a hassle. I am sick of filling these out."

    C. Two guys in dorm room. Guy in doorway: "What's up?"

    D. Teacher: "Let's get started."

Discussion

See the General Teaching Tips, page 7, for suggestions on conducting post-listening discussions.

Part Three: On the Air

Background

English has only one pronoun to use when addressing people: *you*. Students who speak languages with both a formal and an informal second-person pronoun, and students who speak languages with elaborate systems of honorifics, may mistakenly conclude that English is an informal language or that English speakers are rude. Students will learn that in English, we show respect to people by using titles. English also expresses formality in other ways, such as through the use of modal auxiliaries.

A. PRELISTENING (page 14)

Discussion

See the General Teaching Tips, page 3, for suggestions on conducting prelistening speaking activities.

❷ ANSWERS

    1. Informal. "Hey, Kathy" shows that the speaker is probably a friend, social acquaintance, or work colleague who knows Kathy well.

2. Formal. "Ms." is a polite title. The speaker is probably a worker in a doctor's office.

3. Formal. The speakers may be strangers, or the person asking the question may be younger than the listener. "Ma'am" is a title of respect.

4. Informal. "Ma" is an informal way of addressing one's mother.

5. Formal. The speaker is addressing his or her doctor or professor.

Vocabulary Preview

See the General Teaching Tips, page 4, for suggestions on conducting the vocabulary preview.

ANSWERS

1. e	**3.** h	**5.** i	**7.** c	**9.** g
2. d	**4.** f	**6.** b	**8.** a	

B. LISTENING (page 16)

Main Ideas

See the General Teaching Tips, page 4, for suggestions on teaching the Main Ideas section.

❶ ANSWERS

1. title, last name   **3.** Miss or ma'am

2. first name   **4.** title and last name

Details and Inferences

See the General Teaching Tips, page 5, for suggestions on teaching this section.

❸ ANSWERS

1. No	**3.** No	**5.** Yes
2. Yes	**4.** Yes	

Listening for Language

See the General Teaching Tips, page 5, for suggestions on teaching this section.

CONVERSATION TOOLS

1. See the General Teaching Tips, page 6, for suggestions on teaching Conversation Tools.

2. *Note:* The rules presented here are quite formal, and a student would not be wrong if he or she followed them. However, one should remember that levels of formality vary from region to region in the United States and Canada. For example, in California, it is common for people to use each other's first names as soon as they meet, even in business situations.

❻ ANSWERS

1. Miss	**2.** Ms.	**3.** Miss	**4.** Mrs.	**5.** Mr.	**6.** Ms.

C. REAL TALK: USE WHAT YOU'VE LEARNED (page 18)

Vocabulary Review: Discussion

1. See the General Teaching Tips, page 6, for suggestions on teaching this section.
2. The discussion may not generate all the words in the list. In case you don't hear any examples of some items, ask students to make sentences with the missing words after they finish discussing the questions on page 18.

Role Play

See the General Teaching Tips, page 7, for suggestions on conducting role plays.

Part Four: In Class

In this first chapter, spend some time talking to students about the importance and value of learning how to take notes. See the General Teaching Tips, Part Four, page 9.

Art

1. See the General Teaching Tips, page 3, for suggestions on presenting art.
2. Wedding announcements like the one in the Student Book are common in the United States. Typically, an announcement provides the names of the bride and groom, details about the wedding ceremony, and information about the couple's work and family background. The name the bride will use after marriage is also stated.

A. PRELISTENING (page 21)

See the General Teaching Tips, page 9, for suggestions on conducting prelistening activities in this part of the chapter.

Discussion

ANSWERS

1. The husband's name is John Wakesfield.
2. The wife's name is Martha Jude Cox.

Vocabulary Preview

See the General Teaching Tips, page 4, for suggestions on conducting the vocabulary preview.

ANSWERS

1. c	**3.** f	**5.** b	**7.** g
2. h	**4.** e	**6.** d	**8.** a

Pretest

Chapter 1 differs from all the following chapters in that this section begins with a Pretest. The purpose is to provide both you and the student with "baseline" information about the student's ability to take notes. Have students refer back to these notes and evaluate them later, after they begin learning how to take efficient and well-organized notes.

❶ SUGGESTED PROCEDURE

1. Have students take out blank sheets of notebook paper.
2. Read the directions and check to be sure students understand what they are going to do. Reassure them that the purpose of this test is to find out what they already know about taking notes. The test will not be graded. Students should do their best, but they shouldn't worry if they don't understand everything.
3. Remind students that important words—key words—are stressed. They should listen for key words and write those in their notes.
4. Play the recording and observe as students take notes.
5. When the recording is finished, do one of the following:
   - Instruct students to keep their notes and go on to Exercise 2.
   - If the class time is up, collect the notes for safekeeping. Return them to students at the beginning of the next class and have them do Exercise 2 at that time. The advantage of doing this is that students will have forgotten the lecture content and will have to rely on their notes to answer the questions.
   - Have students take their notes home and do Exercise 2 there. *Note:* Do not do this unless you are certain that students will work alone.

❷ SUGGESTED PROCEDURE

1. Read the directions. Decide if you want students to answer the questions in the book or on separate sheets of paper, which you will collect.
2. We provide the answers here, but do not go over them with the students at this time. Tell them that they will have another chance to hear the lecture later and that you'll go over the answers to the questions at that time.

❷ ANSWERS

1. the growing trend among women who choose not to change their names after they get married
2. their husbands'
3. Society became more open and more accepting of people who made untraditional choices.
4. For women it became more acceptable to go to college and have a career.
5. It increased from 8.2 percent in 1970 to 23.6 percent in 2000.
6. The percentage has grown because these women tend to stay in school longer and work for a few years before they get married. They establish an independent professional identity, and they don't want to give it up after marriage.
7. The number of women who don't change their last names will grow.

B. LISTENING AND NOTE-TAKING (page 23)

See the General Teaching Tips, page 9, for suggestions on teaching this section.

Lecture Form: Three Features of Good Notes

See the General Teaching Tips, page 10, for suggestions on teaching this section.

❶ and ❷ SUGGESTED PROCEDURE

1. Read, or call on students to read, the information in the box. As the class reads each feature, have students look at the model notes on the top of page 24.

2. Point out, and continue to remind students throughout the course, that real-world lecture notes are never this perfect. First of all, speakers are not always perfectly organized, so the students' notes will not be perfectly organized either. Second, even experienced note-takers may have difficulty dealing with the content and the form of a lecture at the same time, so that real notes tend to be much messier than this. However, if students plan to use their notes to study for exams, it is to their benefit to copy their notes neatly after every lecture. Copying also gives them a chance to review the lecture content and see if any information is missing.

3. *Optional.* After listening to the lecture, give students a copy of the script for the first part. Read it with the class and have students notice how the Exercise 2 notes compare with the spoken sentences. Also point out sentences or information that isn't included in the notes. Help students to see and understand that notes never include everything the speaker says.

Lecture Language: Statistical Expressions

1. See the General Teaching Tips, page 11, for suggestions on teaching the Lecture Language section.

2. See Appendix 2 on page 208 in the Student Book for a more complete list of common abbreviations and symbols.

❹ ANSWERS

(*Other answers may be correct.*)

Expression	Symbol or Abbreviation
Percent, percentage	%
number	#
less than (1 percent), more than (10 percent)	<(1%), >(10%)
to jump / increase / rise	↑
between (35) and (50)	35-50
(it is) estimated	~

❺ ANSWERS

Note: Students will have approximately 10 seconds to write their notes.
(*Other answers will also be acceptable.*)

1. 1980: 20.9% of Am. men had grad. from college.

2. By 2000: % of men college grads ↑ to 27.8%.

3. 2000: ~98% of Am. schools connected to Internet.

4. There are ~88,000 diff last names in U.S.

5. China: <400 last names.

Call on students to restate their sentences for the whole class. Write their sentences on an overhead transparency. Ask other students to read and evaluate the accuracy of the sentences. Don't expect these sentences to be exactly like those in the lecture. Many paraphrased versions will be acceptable. Errors that do not interfere with meaning can be ignored.

Taking Notes

See the General Teaching Tips, page 11, for suggestions on teaching this section.

❼ PROCEDURE

1. Give students time to look at the incomplete outline before listening.
   Note: As students become more proficient at listening and taking notes, you can skip this step. Have them look at the margin notes and predict what information they will hear.
2. Be sure students close their books and take notes on their own paper.
3. After listening they should use their notes to fill in the outline in their books. If students are confused by this, remind them that in academic classes, students take notes on their own paper, then revise and copy them.

❼ ANSWERS

		III. Relationship between ♀ ed. & name change
trend		♀ go to college → keep name
statistics	◯	Stats
		• 1970: — ‹1% keep name
		• 1980: — 10%
		• 1990 — 23%
		• today — 35-50%
why	◯	IV. Reasons
		1. ed. ♀ marry later →
		2. work before marriage →
		3. don't want to give up profess. identity
conclusion		V. Conc
		• Last 30 yrs: ↑ in % of US ♀ college grads
	◯	↑ in # of ♀ who keep name
		• Total who keep name = 10%
		• Will ↑

(Some variation is acceptable. Check to make sure students indent correctly.)

❽ PROCEDURE

This is a critically important step, so be sure to leave enough time for it.

1. Students can work alone or in pairs. If in pairs, have them look at their partner's notes from the Pretest and from Exercise 7 and try to find improvements in the use of abbreviations and symbols, key words, and indenting.
2. Bring the class back together and call on students to report on the differences between their "before" and "after" notes.

Reviewing the Lecture

1. See the General Teaching Tips, page 12, for suggestions on conducting this activity.
2. *Optional.* Hand out the lecture script after students finish going over the Pretest questions. See Using the Audioscript on page 13 of the General Teaching Tips.

C. REAL TALK: USE WHAT YOU'VE LEARNED (page 26)

See the General Teaching Tips, page 13, for suggestions on teaching this section.

Vocabulary Review: Discussion

See the General Teaching Tips, page 6, for suggestions on teaching this section.

Practice with Statistics

See the General Teaching Tips, page 9, for suggestions on conducting information gap activities.

❸ ANSWER

The percentage of women PhD's increased from 13.5 in 1970 to 44 in 2000. / It increased more than three times.

LET'S GET AWAY!

Part One: In Person

Art

See the General Teaching Tips, page 3, for suggestions on presenting art.

A. PRELISTENING (page 28)

Discussion

1. See the General Teaching Tips, page 3, for suggestions on conducting prelistening speaking activities.
2. The woman is waiting for luggage at an airport. The man is looking at his car's tire and calling for help; the weather seems cold.

Vocabulary Preview

See the General Teaching Tips, page 4, for suggestions on conducting the vocabulary preview.

ANSWERS

1. j	**3.** e	**5.** b	**7.** a	**9.** c
2. d	**4.** f	**6.** g	**8.** i	**10.** h

B. LISTENING (page 30)
Main Ideas

1. The expression *pet peeve* means "something that annoys you very much." Students should have no trouble guessing the meaning from the listening segments as the speakers talk about the things that annoy them the most about traveling. Therefore, do not provide the meaning of *pet peeve* before the listening activity. Rather, ask students to define this term after they've listened to all the segments. Other acceptable definitions are "something that always bothers you," "some behavior that you don't like or that upsets you."
2. Speaker 2 mentions ATMs (automated teller machines). While most students are familiar with ATM machines, they may know them by the name of *cash machine*, *bank machine*, or *cash point*, as they are called in some other English-speaking countries.
3. See the General Teaching Tips, page 4, for suggestions on teaching the Main Ideas section.

❶ SUGGESTED ANSWERS

(Wording may vary.)

Speaker 1: waiting for other people; when a group has to wait for one person who is late
Speaker 2: not finding an ATM machine, having to exchange money at a hotel and paying a higher exchange rate
Speaker 3: can't have scissors in carry-on baggage
Speaker 4: everything getting messed up and wrinkled in the bag after being searched, can't zip the bag

Details and Inferences

See the General Teaching Tips, page 5, for suggestions on teaching this section.

❷ ANSWERS

Speaker 1
1. I   **2.** I

Speaker 2
3. T   **4.** T

Speaker 3
5. T   **6.** T
7. F   **8.** I

Speaker 4
9. T   **10.** I

Listening for Language

See the General Teaching Tips, page 5, for suggestions on teaching this section.

FOCUS ON SOUND

See the General Teaching Tips, page 5, for suggestions on teaching Focus on Sound.

❹ ANSWERS

1. can't stand about traveling
2. a group of people
3. part of the day
4. in a hurry
5. travel overseas
6. find an ATM
7. when I travel
8. spend a lot of time
9. take out everything
10. it's impossible

❺ ANSWERS

1. I end up feeling really ripped off and . . . well, irritated.
2. It is impossible for me to carry my scissors.
3. You get picked out of line for one of the random searches.

4. They take out everything that you spent so much time putting in place so carefully.

5. Everything is all wrinkled and messed up.

CONVERSATION TOOLS

See the General Teaching Tips, page 6, for suggestions on teaching Conversation Tools.

⑦ ANSWERS

Speaker <u>3</u>: ticks me off
Speaker <u>1</u>: can't stand
Speaker <u>4</u>: hate
Speaker <u>2</u>: is irritating
Speaker <u>2</u>: feel irritated

C. REAL TALK: USE WHAT YOU'VE LEARNED (page 33)

Vocabulary Review: Discussion

See the General Teaching Tips, page 6, for suggestions on conducting the vocabulary review.

Interview

See the General Teaching Tips, page 8, for suggestions on conducting the interview. *Note: Rank order* means to organize details from largest to smallest, from most to least frequent, etc.

Part Two: On the Phone

Art

See the General Teaching Tips, page 3, for suggestions on presenting art.

A. PRELISTENING (page 34)

Discussion

See the General Teaching Tips, page 3, for suggestions on conducting prelistening speaking activities.

POSSIBLE ANSWERS

Customer

How much is the fare? What time does the plane depart/arrive? Is it a nonstop flight?

Agent

When do you want to travel? How many passengers are traveling? Do you want to fly coach or first class? Do you want a morning or afternoon flight?

Vocabulary Preview

See the General Teaching Tips, page 4, for suggestions on conducting the vocabulary preview.

B. LISTENING (page 35)

Main Ideas

See the General Teaching Tips, page 4, for suggestions on teaching the Main Ideas section.

❶ ANSWERS

1. F	**3.** T	**5.** T
2. T	**4.** F	

Details and Inferences

See the General Teaching Tips, page 5, for suggestions on teaching this section.

❷ ANSWERS

```
FOR: DOMANICK   JOANNE
ADDRESS: 10920 WILSHIRE BLVD.
PHONE:     555-1212
FAX:       555-3213
AIR TRANSPORTATION:     $  379.37
```

DEPART FROM	DATE	AIRLINE	TIME	ARRIVE IN
LA	Sept 8	United	11:25	New York

RETURN TRIP

New York	Sept 13	United	4:15	LA

```
EQUIPMENT:   BOEING 767      AIR MILES: 4950 miles round trip
CLASS:       COACH           AGENT:  MARK
```

Listening for Language

See the General Teaching Tips, page 5, for suggestions on teaching this section.

❸ ANSWERS

1. looking at
2. could if it
3. for any; tickets are issued
4. purchase it; four hours
5. got a
6. hang on a

C. REAL TALK: USE WHAT YOU'VE LEARNED (page 37)

Vocabulary Review: Discussion

See the General Teaching Tips, page 6, for suggestions on conducting the vocabulary review.

Problem Solving

1. Have students read each situation silently and choose a solution.
2. Have students sit in pairs or groups and discuss their choices. Be sure they explain their reasons.
3. Bring the class together and have them share their decisions.
4. Ask students if they or someone they know has ever experienced a similar situation or decision.

Part Three: On the Air

Art

See the General Teaching Tips, page 3, for suggestions on presenting art.

A. PRELISTENING (page 38)

Discussion

See the General Teaching Tips, page 3, for suggestions on conducting prelistening speaking activities.

Vocabulary Preview

See the General Teaching Tips, page 4, for suggestions on conducting the vocabulary preview.

ANSWERS

1. c	3. g	5. j	7. b	9. d
2. a	4. f	6. e	8. h	10. i

B. LISTENING (page 40)

Main Ideas

See the General Teaching Tips, page 4, for suggestions on teaching the Main Ideas section.

❶ NOTE

After reading the information about "The Five W's," ask students to give an example of a recent news event. Have them summarize it based on the five W's.

❷ NOTE

News reports tend to be difficult to comprehend because they are information-dense and are normally delivered at a fast rate of speech. For these reasons, this exercise will most likely be challenging for your students. To help them separate the main ideas from the details, remind them that each segment will consist of (a) a news event and (b) some advice for travelers. For this exercise, have students focus on the main idea, i.e., the news event. Replay the segments several times until students are able to separate what happened from the advice given as a result of the event.

❷ ANSWERS

Who/What is the story about?	What happened?	Where did it happen?	When did it happen?	Why did it happen?
1. 100 mountain climbers	Climbers died in accidents	the Alps	since the end of June	X
2. health officials	warned people	Florida	this week	mosquitoes found; outbreak of disease possible
3. airline crash	killed 200+ people	Indonesia	this week	smog from burning forests, poor visibility
4. problem for travelers	lack of hotel rooms	Tokyo	this month	many visitors at Olympic games

Details and Inferences

See the General Teaching Tips, page 5, for suggestions on teaching this section.

❸ ANSWERS

1. T	**4.** T	**7.** F
2. F	**5.** T	**8.** F
3. T	**6.** T	**9.** F

Listening for Language

See the General Teaching Tips, page 5, for suggestions on teaching this section.

CONVERSATION TOOLS

See the General Teaching Tips, page 6, for suggestions on teaching Conversation Tools.

❺ ANSWERS

1. urged; to take
2. Cover up; use; advice
3. recommend staying
4. has been urging; to stay
5. book

C. REAL TALK: USE WHAT YOU'VE LEARNED (page 42)

Vocabulary Review: News Reports

See the General Teaching Tips, page 6, for suggestions on conducting the vocabulary review. *Note:* This activity requires that students retell (summarize) the news reports in their own words. Students may look at their notes from Exercise 2 on page 40 as well as the vocabulary box on page 42.

Role Play

See the General Teaching Tips, page 7, for suggestions on conducting role plays.

Part Four: In Class

A. PRELISTENING (page 44)

See the General Teaching Tips, page 9, for suggestions on conducting prelistening speaking activities.

Vocabulary Preview

See the General Teaching Tips, page 4, for suggestions on conducting the vocabulary preview.

ANSWERS

1. c	**3.** a	**5.** d	**7.** e	**9.** j
2. i	**4.** h	**6.** b	**8.** f	**10.** g

B. LISTENING AND NOTE-TAKING (page 45)

Lecture Organization: Introductions

See the General Teaching Tips, page 9, for suggestions on teaching this section.

❷ NOTE

Discuss the correct answers with the class or have pairs of students share their answers. Have students justify their answer choices.

❷ ANSWERS
1. M (The speaker says they've already talked about phobias, so it was probably defined previously. However, the speaker may repeat the definition to help students remember.)
2. Y (The speaker clearly says she wants to focus on one common phobia.)
3. N (The speaker says she is *not* going to go into the causes.)
4. M (The speaker is going to focus on treatment; this may involve getting help from friends.)
5. Y (The focus is going to be on *treatment,* which by definition is given by professionals.)
6. N (The speaker says she is *not* going to talk about the symptoms.)

Lecture Language: Defining Terms

See the General Teaching Tips, page 11, for suggestions on teaching this section.

❹ ANSWERS

Term	Definition
1. panic	sudden, uncontrollable fear → great confusion, desire to escape
2. psychiatry	branch of medicine; study & treatment of mental illness
3. psychology	study of mind; treatment of behavior disorders / problems
4. psycho	mentally disturbed, sick (slang—neg. meaning; insulting; person acting crazy)

Taking Notes

See the General Teaching Tips, page 11, for suggestions on teaching this section. *Note:* The speaker in this lecture refers to the handout on page 49: "Harry's List of Feared Situations." Have students study the handout for a few minutes before they listen. As you play the lecture, pause the recording for a few moments when the speaker says, "You can see Harry's list on your handout" and check to make sure that everyone is looking at the information on the list.

introduction		Common phobia: Fear of flying
		Focus on treatment
	◯	
definition of phobia		Phobia: intense, irrational fear
		Fear of flying — unrealistic but common
details / statistics about fear of flying		• plane travel = 20 x safer than car travel
		• yet 25 mil. Americans have aerophobia
what can help?		Treatment: behavior therapy — "desensitization" to make you less sensitive
		In therapist's office
		Phase 1: progressive relaxation
		relax muscles → control body →
	◯	eliminate anxiety
		Phase 2: make list of frightening situations,
		rating anxiety levels
		Phase 3: imagine each situation and relax
		In the real world (phase 4): experience situations in real life — actually do things on list
		1st day: take friend to airport, go home
		2nd day: go to airport, walk in
		3rd day: go to airport, go through metal detector
		use relaxation technique to feel
		comfortable
conclusion	◯	Conc:
		Total treatment = 2 mos.
		Desens. cured Harry's phobia

Reviewing the Lecture

See the General Teaching Tips, page 12, for suggestions on teaching this section.

C. REAL TALK: USE WHAT YOU'VE LEARNED (PAGE 49)

See the General Teaching Tips, page 13, for suggestions on teaching this section.

CHAPTER 3

LOOKING FOR LOVE

Part One: In Person

Background

In the 1950s, relationships between people of different races or religions were very rare in the United States, and they were viewed with disapproval or even shock. In the last 40 years there has been a gradual change of attitude. Nowadays relationships between people from different backgrounds are more common, especially in large cities, although there are still families that disapprove of their children marrying someone from a different racial, religious, or social background.

Art

The photo shows an Asian man and a woman who might be Caucasian or possibly Latin (i.e., from a Spanish-speaking background). See the General Teaching Tips, page 3, for suggestions on presenting art.

A. PRELISTENING (page 51)

Discussion

See the General Teaching Tips, page 3, for suggestions on conducting prelistening speaking activities.

Vocabulary Preview

See the General Teaching Tips, page 4, for suggestions on conducting the vocabulary preview.

ANSWERS

1. f	**3.** a	**5.** e	**7.** b
2. h	**4.** g	**6.** c	**8.** d

B. LISTENING (page 52)

Main Ideas

See the General Teaching Tips, page 4, for suggestions on teaching the Main Ideas section.

🕐 ANSWERS

1. How do you think your parents would feel if you married someone who wasn't Korean?
2. Her mother is concerned that if she married someone who wasn't Korean, her husband would feel left out at family gatherings. Her father stays out of it.
3. How would your parents feel if you married someone who wasn't of the same religion?

4. He doesn't answer her question directly. Instead, he gives his own opinion. He says he would not marry someone of a different religion.

5. Different. Kathy would marry someone from a different background, but Mark would not marry someone with a different religion.

Details and Inferences

1. See the General Teaching Tips, page 5, for suggestions on teaching this section.

2. After listening and going over the answers, you might want to have students say which speaker they agree with and explain why they feel that way.

❷ **ANSWERS**

Person	Attitude	Reason (if given)
1. Kathy—past	(for) / against / no opinion	She feels more American than Korean.
2. Kathy's mother	for / (against) / no opinion	Kathy's aunt married a Caucasian man, and her mother worried that he felt left out at family gatherings.
3. Kathy's father	for / against / (no opinion)	
4. Kathy—now	for / (against) / no opinion	She wants her husband to have a close relationship with her parents.
5. Mark	for / (against) / no opinion	Married people can avoid a lot of problems if they have the same beliefs. His religion is a very important part of who he is.

Listening for Language

1. See the General Teaching Tips, page 5, for suggestions on teaching this section.

2. Students usually enjoy trying to pronounce reduced forms. Encourage them, but also tell them that it is not really necessary for them to learn how to speak with a native-like accent. It is much more important for them to learn to *understand* the speech of native speakers when they hear it.

FOCUS ON SOUND

See the General Teaching Tips, page 5, for suggestions on teaching Focus on Sound.

1. How do you feel about your English class?
2. It's probably going to rain this evening.
3. My goal is to learn how to speak, read, and write Spanish.
4. Jane's new boyfriend is kind of quiet.
5. My parents would feel bad if I married a person with a different religion.

C. REAL TALK: USE WHAT YOU'VE LEARNED (page 55)

Vocabulary Review: Discussion

See the General Teaching Tips, page 6, for suggestions on conducting the vocabulary review.

❶ ANSWERS

(Answers will vary according to students' opinions.)

Part Two: On the Phone

Art

See the General Teaching Tips, page 3, for suggestions on presenting art.

A. PRELISTENING (page 56)

Discussion

1. See the General Teaching Tips, page 3, for suggestions on conducting prelistening speaking activities.
2. The word *mate* is used in the directions to include both married and unmarried couples.
3. In the United States, the most common way for people to meet their mates is through personal introductions by family or friends. All the other ways in the list are also common. Matchmaking services are usually companies that use technology such as computers and videotapes to match people up. A matchmaker provides more personal service to individuals looking for a mate.

Vocabulary Preview

See the General Teaching Tips, page 4, for suggestions on conducting the vocabulary preview.

ANSWERS

1. d	**3.** f	**5.** a	**7.** g	**9.** e
2. i	**4.** b	**6.** h	**8.** c	

B. LISTENING (page 58)

Main Ideas

See the General Teaching Tips, page 4, for suggestions on teaching the Main Ideas section.

❶ ANSWERS

Information about	
Jay	**Bright Futures**
Reason for call: To get information	Type of service: Private membership club for singles
Referred by: A friend	History: More than 10 years old.
Age: 28	Size: 8,000 members
Occupation: Advertising	How it works: They have a library with profiles, photos, and videos.
Final decision: He will call them back when he is ready to make an appointment.	Cost: No info

Details and Inferences

See the General Teaching Tips, page 5, for suggestions on teaching this section.

❸ ANSWERS

1. b   3. a
2. b   4. c

❹ ANSWERS

Adjectives to describe Jay: embarrassed, hesitant, polite, shy, funny, lonely

Adjectives to describe Linda: confident, aggressive, energetic, enthusiastic

Listening for Language

See the General Teaching Tips, page 5, for suggestions on teaching this section.

CONVERSATION TOOLS

See the General Teaching Tips, page 6, for suggestions on teaching Conversation Tools.

❺ ANSWERS

1. I don't mean to interrupt, but . . .
2. Can I just jump in here?

See the General Teaching Tips, page 5, for suggestions on teaching Focus on Sound.

⑧ ANSWERS

1. we; you	**3.** everybody	**5.** do
2. other; hadn't	**4.** you; us	

C. REAL TALK: USE WHAT YOU'VE LEARNED (page 61)

Vocabulary Review: Conversation

See the General Teaching Tips, page 6, for suggestions on conducting the vocabulary review.

ANSWERS

1. pool	**4.** screen	**7.** hook
2. every single one	**5.** profile	**8.** ballpark figure
3. match people up	**6.** chemistry	**9.** keep in mind

Interrupting Game

1. Read the directions with the students.
2. Review the Conversation Tools on page 59 of the Student Book. Encourage students to use a variety of expressions as they speak.
3. Model the activity with a volunteer.
4. Circulate as students are talking. Correct errors in the use of interrupting phrases, and remind students to use a variety of expressions.
5. You may wish to note other errors you hear and go over them with the class after they finish speaking.

Part Three: On the Air

Art

1. See the General Teaching Tips, page 3, for suggestions on presenting art.
2. Make sure students notice that the people in these pictures are doing things alone.

A. PRELISTENING (page 63)

Prediction

1. See the General Teaching Tips, page 3, for suggestions on conducting prelistening speaking activities.
2. *Possible answers:*

   People may choose to stay single because

   * They value their freedom over the desire to be with a partner.
   * They may have been unhappily married and do not want to make the same mistake again.
   * They may love their work passionately and may not have time for a spouse.

- They may not have found the right person to marry.
- They may be homosexual.
- They feel they can't afford to get married.

People may choose to get married because

- They are in love.
- Society or their families expect them to do so.
- They want to have children.
- They want to be with someone who can support them financially.
- They want status.

Vocabulary Preview

See the General Teaching Tips, page 4, for suggestions on conducting the vocabulary preview.

ANSWERS

1. e	**3.** g	**5.** f	**7.** c
2. h	**4.** b	**6.** a	**8.** d

B. LISTENING (page 65)

Main Ideas

See the General Teaching Tips, page 4, for suggestions on teaching the Main Ideas section.

❶ ANSWERS

	Age	Reasons for Choosing to Stay Single
Neil L.	fifty-two	He likes his:
		1. freedom
		2. independence
		3. privacy
		4. solitude
Jennifer S.	thirty-one	She isn't sure whether she wants to get married or have kids.
Terri W.	early fifties	1. She doesn't feel pressure to marry because she doesn't want children.
		2. Doesn't need a committed relationship to feel fulfilled.

❷ ANSWERS

Answers will vary. Students should compare their answers from the Prelistening activity with the answers to Exercise 1 above.

Details and Inferences

See the General Teaching Tips, page 5, for suggestions on teaching this section.

③ ANSWERS

1. F (He has been in a committed relationship for ten years.)

2. F (He says he is not against marriage.)

3. T (She says she is "not sure" whether she wants to get married and have kids.)

4. F (Most of her friends are "desperately" seeking someone.)

5. F (She says she gets lonely just like everyone else.)

6. T (She says this.)

Listening for Language

See the General Teaching Tips, page 5, for suggestions on teaching this section.

CONVERSATION TOOLS

See the General Teaching Tips, page 6, for suggestions on teaching Conversation Tools.

⑤ ANSWERS

. . . (she) wonders about (marriage all the time).

(I'm) not sure whether (I want to get married or not . . .)

(I'm) not sure of (the benefits of getting married).

C. REAL TALK: USE WHAT YOU'VE LEARNED (page 66)

Vocabulary Review: Discussion

See the General Teaching Tips, page 6, for suggestions on conducting the vocabulary review.

Expressing Doubts

1. Read the directions with the students.
2. Put students in pairs or small groups.
3. Model one or two sentences, for example:

Lisa wonders if Greg will love her child.
Greg isn't sure he is ready to get married.

4. Circulate as students are talking. Correct errors in structures for expressing doubt.
5. You may wish to note other errors you hear and go over them with the class after they finish speaking.

POSSIBLE ANSWERS

Lisa wonders if Greg really wants to get married.
Lisa doesn't know if Greg will be a good stepfather.
Lisa wonders if Greg will feel bad that she earns more money than he does.
Lisa wonders why Greg has never been married before.

Greg wonders if Lisa will be happy if she is married to him.

Greg isn't sure he wants to get married.

Greg wonders if he will be a good father.

Group Presentation

1. Read the directions with the students and group them accordingly. If possible, create groups with men and women together.
2. Have students create the worksheet on their own paper. The chart in the book is only a model.
3. If your class is large, groups can present their ideas to other groups instead of the whole class. However, bring everyone back together at the end for the class vote.

Part Four: In Class

Art

1. See the General Teaching Tips, page 3, for suggestions on presenting art.
2. Testosterone, dopamine, and oxytocin are brain chemicals that play a part in the process of attraction between males and females. These terms are defined in the lecture.

A. PRELISTENING (page 68)

Discussion

See the General Teaching Tips, page 9, for suggestions on conducting prelistening speaking activities.

ANSWER

1. The couple's idea of love is romantic. They are daydreaming about the symbols of romantic love. The scientist's idea of love is clinical, analytical, scientific. He thinks of love as a chemical or biological process.

Vocabulary Preview

See the General Teaching Tips, page 4, for suggestions on conducting the vocabulary preview.

ANSWERS

1. f	**3.** e	**5.** a	**7.** c
2. h	**4.** g	**6.** d	**8.** b

B. LISTENING AND NOTE-TAKING (page 70)

Lecture Organization: Transitions

See the General Teaching Tips, page 10, for suggestions on teaching this section.

1. The first stage	**4.** First	**7.** let's review
2. the second phase of love	**5.** In contrast	
3. For example	**6.** Now	

Lecture Form: Outlining

1. See the General Teaching Tips, page 10, for suggestions on teaching this section.
2. Once again point out to students that real lecture notes are never as neat as the model on page 72 of the Student Book. In fact, real notes tend to be quite messy. An excellent way to review a lecture, however, is to copy one's notes in outline form. This (a) helps students remember the lecture content and (b) makes the notes easier to read when it is time to study for exams.
3. *Note:* Students in U.S. universities *must* learn how to understand and use outlines. Many professors require students to turn in outlines of research projects, articles they have read, etc. Also, professors often provide outlines for lectures or courses.

Taking Notes

See the General Teaching Tips, page 11, for suggestions on teaching this section. Be sure to follow the instructions in the book. Students should take notes on their own paper, then edit them and complete the outline in the book.

SAMPLE NOTES

introduction	I. Topic: The biology of love
	Love = bio process
stages	II. Dr. Helen Fisher (Rutgers U.): love →
	3 stages w/diff. chemicals active in brain
1st stage	A. Lust
definition	1. powerful sexual attract. to another person
hormone	2. hormone = testosterone
	a. not just male hormone
	b. → sex drive in men & women
2nd stage	B. Romantic love
characteristics	1. become emotionally attached
	2. feel passionate, romantic, madly in love
hormone	3. brain chemical = dopamine

research study	4. study @ U. of London
1st step	a. volunteers saw pics of lovers
2nd step	b. saw pics of friends
	c. sci. used MRI to record brain activ.
results	5. when vol. saw pic. of lovers → part of brain that
	makes dopamine (pleasure hormone) very active
	when pic. of friends → no activity
conclusion	6. conc.: dopamine essential for romantic phase
	of love
3rd stage	C. Attachment phase
characteristics	1. people settle down, have children
	2. feelings = peace, security, stability
hormone	3. important hormone = oxytocin
animal research	a. animals that rec'd it attached quickly to
	partners
	b. if hormone blocked → showed no interest
humans	c. humans: found in blood of men & women in
	stable relationships
role of oxytocin	4. scientists think oxy. may play imp. role in ability
	to form close relat.
conclusion	
	III. Real organ of love: brain not heart
	Love = bio. process like eating, etc.

Reviewing the Lecture

1. See the General Teaching Tips, page 12, for suggestions on teaching this section.
2. Give students a copy of the Audioscript, if you choose.

C. REAL TALK: USE WHAT YOU'VE LEARNED (page 74)

See the General Teaching Tips, page 13, for suggestions on teaching this section.

Vocabulary Review: Discussion

See the General Teaching Tips, page 6, for suggestions on teaching this section.

Expansion: Love Idioms

1. If an English speaker is not available for students to interview, they may find the meaning of these idioms on the Internet. For example, a search for "*love at first sight*" + *idiom* + *definition* yields several websites that define the idiom. Other useful search terms are *English* + *idioms, idioms* + *English,* "*idioms index.*" Remind students to use quotation marks as shown.

2. *Note:* The distinction between lust and romantic love is not always clear. "Love at first sight" could probably go under both categories, depending on whether the feeling was more sexual (lust) or emotional (romantic love).

Lust	Romantic Love	Attachment
Be/Get turned on	Fall head over heels in love	Settle down
Have an affair	Go steady	Make a commitment
Love at first sight	Have a crush on somebody	Tie the knot
	Puppy love	
	Sweep someone off his/her feet	
	(Be) madly in love	

CHAPTER 4	MUSIC TO MY EARS

Part One: In Person

Art

See the General Teaching Tips, page 3, for suggestions on presenting art.

A. PRELISTENING (page 76)

Discussion

1. See the General Teaching Tips, page 3, for suggestions on conducting prelistening speaking activities.
2. Besides the example given on page 76 of the Student Book, other types of music to discuss are jazz, classical, pop, rock, and hip-hop. If students have difficulty describing the characteristics of each genre, have them choose their favorite kind and describe it. If students lack sufficient vocabulary, remind them that this chapter will teach many common music-related words and expressions.

Vocabulary Preview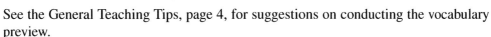

See the General Teaching Tips, page 4, for suggestions on conducting the vocabulary preview.

ANSWERS

1. b	**3.** d	**5.** f	**7.** h
2. e	**4.** g	**6.** a	**8.** c

B. LISTENING (page 78)

Main Ideas

See the General Teaching Tips, page 4, for suggestions on teaching the Main Ideas section.

❶ ANSWERS

Speaker	Favorite type(s) of music	Why he/she likes it
1. Sarah	jazz	—can be fast, slow, soft, loud —different rhythms —lots of different instruments
2. Kathleen	bossa nova	—soothing —inspiring —subtle, soft —rhythmic

(continued)

Speaker	Favorite type(s) of music	Why he/she likes it
3. Bonnie	classical	—has orchestra, chorus —diff. kinds of instruments, esp. strings (her favorite)
4. Dennis	folk	—down-to-earth —honest, not overproduced —very American —likes acoustic instruments
5. Andrea	rock	—can feel connection to lyrics
6. Spencer	ska	—upbeat character —likes the beat (drums) —fun

Details and Inferences

See the General Teaching Tips, page 5, for suggestions on teaching this section.

❷ ANSWERS

1. Dennis	**3.** Bonnie	**5.** Sarah
2. Spencer	**4.** Kathleen	**6.** Bonnie

Listening for Language

See the General Teaching Tips, page 5, for suggestions on teaching this section.

CONVERSATION TOOLS

1. See the General Teaching Tips, page 6, for suggestions on teaching this section.
2. To help students better understand the concepts of connotation and denotation, you may want to give additional examples, such as
   - slender (+), skinny (–), thin (0)
   - to chat (+), to gossip (–), to talk (0)
3. When learning new vocabulary, students need to pay attention to the context or ask a native speaker to find out about the connotation. In addition, most dictionaries, such as the *Longman Dictionary of American English,* provide usage labels like *slang* and *taboo.* Exercise 5 provides practice in guessing the connotation of adjectives from context. Have students point out specific clues in the context that helped them choose the right answer.

❺ ANSWERS

1. _0_ loud	_0_ soft	_0_ fast	_0_ slow
2. _+_ subtle	_+_ soft	_+_ rhythmic	_+_ soothing
3. _+_ down-to-earth	_+_ honest	_–_ overproduced	
4. _–_ loud	_–_ screaming		

C. REAL TALK: USE WHAT YOU'VE LEARNED (page 80)

Vocabulary Review: Discussion

See the General Teaching Tips, page 6, for suggestions on conducting the vocabulary review.

Oral Presentation

This activity works best when students are allowed to prepare their presentations at home. Encourage students to bring recordings of their favorite music to class; this will liven up their presentations as well as help the audience understand the type of music being described.

SUGGESTED PROCEDURE

1. Check to make sure audio equipment is available and is in working order before students give their presentations.
2. Allow students to speak from notes but without reading prewritten paragraphs.
3. Prepare the rest of the class (the audience) to listen actively. Have them take notes during the presentations and ask the presenter follow-up questions.

Survey

See the General Teaching Tips, page 8, for suggestions on teaching this activity.

Part Two: On the Phone

Background

Ticketmaster is the world's largest ticketing company. It sells tickets to concerts and other entertainment events over the phone and via the Internet. Ticketmaster is based in West Hollywood, California, but it has operations in many countries around the world.

A. PRELISTENING (page 81)

Discussion

See the General Teaching Tips, page 3, for suggestions on conducting prelistening speaking activities.

Vocabulary Preview

See the General Teaching Tips, page 4, for suggestions on conducting the vocabulary preview.

ANSWERS

1. g	**3.** d	**5.** f	**7.** a
2. h	**4.** c	**6.** e	**8.** b

B. LISTENING (page 82)

Main Ideas

See the General Teaching Tips, page 4, for suggestions on teaching the Main Ideas section.

❶ ANSWERS

1. university ticket office

2. are

3. won't

4. hasn't

Details and Inferences

See the General Teaching Tips, page 5, for suggestions on teaching this section.

❷ ANSWERS

1. a	**3.** a—1	**4.** a	**6.** b
2. c	b—3	**5.** b	
	c—2		

Listening for Language

See the General Teaching Tips, page 5, for suggestions on teaching this section.

FOCUS ON SOUND

See the General Teaching Tips, page 5, for suggestions on teaching Focus on Sound.

❹ ANSWERS

1. wébsite

2. óffice hours

3. tícket prices

4. órchestra level

5. réfund policy

❺ ANSWERS

róck music

níghtclub

músic teacher

tápe recorder

CD player

stríng instruments

cóncert hall

piáno lesson

jázz musician

rádio station

C. REAL TALK: USE WHAT YOU'VE LEARNED (page 84)

Vocabulary Review: Pair Interview

1. See the General Teaching Tips, page 6, for suggestions on conducting the vocabulary review.
2. To conduct the pair interview, have students take turns asking one question each. Or they may ask all three of their questions in a row.

Role Play

See General Teaching Tips, page 7, for suggestions on conducting role plays.

SAMPLE QUESTIONS FOR CALLER

What are the concert dates? / Which dates is Coldplay playing? / When is Coldplay playing?
What are the show times? / When does the concert start?
What are the ticket prices? / How much are the tickets?
Where are the seats? / What's the location of the seats?
What's your refund policy? / Can I return the tickets?

Part Three: On the Air

Art

See the General Teaching Tips, page 3, for suggestions on presenting art.

A. PRELISTENING (page 87)

Discussion

See the General Teaching Tips, page 3, for suggestions on conducting prelistening speaking activities.

Vocabulary Preview

See the General Teaching Tips, page 4, for suggestions on conducting the vocabulary preview.

ANSWERS

1. h	**3.** f	**5.** a	**7.** d	**9.** j
2. c	**4.** g	**6.** b	**8.** e	**10.** i

B. LISTENING (page 88)

Main Ideas

See the General Teaching Tips, page 4, for suggestions on teaching the Main Ideas section.

🔘 ANSWERS

(*Wording may vary.*)

1. Take legal action against people who illegally share music files on the Internet / Threaten to take to court people who illegally share music files on the Internet
2. They don't worry about it / They are not afraid / They don't care

Details and Inferences

See the General Teaching Tips, page 5, for suggestions on teaching this section.

❷ ANSWERS

   1. c   **2.** a   **3.** b   **4.** b

Listening for Language

See the General Teaching Tips, page 5, for suggestions on teaching this section.

FOCUS ON SOUND

See the General Teaching Tips, page 5, for suggestions on teaching Focus on Sound.

❹ ANSWERS

   1. come áfter   **3.** turn óff   **5.** shrug óff

   2. pull óut of   **4.** come óut   **6.** crack dówn on

❺ ANSWERS

   1. Christian isn't worried that the <u>music compánies</u> will <u>come áfter</u> him for sharing <u>músic files</u>.

   2. Satoshi <u>turned óff</u> the MP3 player that he <u>pulled óut of</u> his pocket.

   3. The <u>recórding industry</u> can't <u>crack dówn on</u> millions of <u>IP addrésses</u>.

   4. <u>Músic fans</u> just <u>shrug óff</u> the threat of <u>láwsuits</u>.

C. REAL TALK: USE WHAT YOU'VE LEARNED (page 90)

Vocabulary Review: Discussion

See the General Teaching Tips, page 6, for suggestions on conducting the vocabulary review.

Mock Trial

Students must separate into three groups: those who support file sharing (Judy's lawyers), those who are against it (the recording company's lawyers), and the judges.

SUGGESTED PROCEDURES

   1. To assign students to a particular group, use one of these options:

      a. Arbitrarily divide the class into three equal groups.

      b. Let the students decide which group to join, according to their feeling about the issue of file sharing.

      c. Assign students to the group representing the view opposite their real one; allow undecided or reticent students to be the "judges."

2. While the two groups of "lawyers" prepare their arguments, assign a topic for the "judges" to discuss, for example, "Discuss your definition of 'stealing'" or "Prepare some questions you would like to ask the lawyers on either side."

3. During the trial, you may want to take the role of "court reporter" and take notes on the board. This will help keep track of all the arguments and make it easier for the "judges" to make their decision.

Part Four: In Class

Art

1. See the General Teaching Tips, page 3, for suggestions on presenting art.
2. Ask students if they know who the rap artist is in the picture (Eminem) and how much they know about his music.

A. PRELISTENING (page 92)

See the General Teaching Tips, page 9, for suggestions on conducting prelistening speaking activities.

Quiz: *Rap Music*

The purpose of this quiz is not to test but to activate students' prior knowledge about the characteristics and history of rap music. It should be enjoyable. Encourage students to guess the answers if they are not familiar with this topic.

SUGGESTED PROCEDURES

1. Have students answer the questions individually, either in class or at home.
2. Have students compare their answers in groups *before* checking the answer key. Encourage students to discuss differences between their answers and the reasons for their choices.
3. Have students check the answer key on page 99 of the Student Book and discuss any surprising information.

Vocabulary Preview

See the General Teaching Tips, page 4, for suggestions on conducting the vocabulary preview.

ANSWERS

1. b	**4.** i	**7.** f
2. h	**5.** a	**8.** g
3. d	**6.** e	**9.** c

B. LISTENING AND NOTE-TAKING (page 94)

Lecture Organization: Classifying

See the General Teaching Tips, page 10, for suggestions on teaching this section.

❷ **ANSWERS**

b. rap lyrics: (a) gangsta rap, (b) soft-core

c. 20+ kinds of rap, e.g., comedy rap, pop rap, electro, etc.

d. Latin dancing: salsa, samba, tango

Lecture Language: Paraphrasing

See the General Teaching Tips, page 11, for suggestions on teaching this section.

❹ **ANSWERS**

1. In other words	**3.** I mean
2. That is to say	**4.** or

Taking Notes

See the General Teaching Tips, page 11, for suggestions on teaching this section.

SAMPLE OUTLINE

introduction		Topic: Rap
		Why easy to recognize? Distinctive characteristics
	◯	
definition		Rap: genre of music
(2 components)		2 components
		• rhyming lyrics
		• musical backgr./accompaniment
origins of rap		1970s: –started in NYC by young, poor Afr. Americans
		–used turntable
	◯	–unique element: "scratching" (= unusual sound
		by moving record w/hand on turntable)
		Musical elements today:
		more sophisticated
		1. background melody (tune) can sing, can create
		w/any instrument
	◯	2. backbeat (most prominent) (rhythm)
		repetitive drum sound
		3. sampling = take piece of recording + use in new
		recording, e.g. Coolio's song used classical recording

<table>
<tr><td>other
components
of rap</td><td></td><td>Lyrics:</td></tr>
<tr><td></td><td></td><td>1. gangsta rap</td></tr>
<tr><td></td><td>○</td><td>-early '80s</td></tr>
<tr><td></td><td></td><td>-form of protest, frustration at difficulties,</td></tr>
<tr><td></td><td></td><td> realities of life (drugs, gangs, guns, violence)</td></tr>
<tr><td></td><td></td><td>-shocking language, speak about women in neg. way</td></tr>
<tr><td></td><td></td><td>2. soft-core</td></tr>
<tr><td></td><td></td><td>-mid-90s</td></tr>
<tr><td></td><td></td><td>-less violent</td></tr>
<tr><td></td><td></td><td>-still emphasized money, cars, jewelry</td></tr>
<tr><td></td><td>○</td><td>These days:</td></tr>
<tr><td></td><td></td><td>-lyrics → more positive messages</td></tr>
<tr><td></td><td></td><td>-rap → mainstream, e.g.:</td></tr>
<tr><td></td><td></td><td>• rap artists in movies</td></tr>
<tr><td></td><td></td><td>• co's use rap to sell products</td></tr>
<tr><td></td><td></td><td>• France: rap = officially "art"; 2nd
  largest market for rap</td></tr>
<tr><td></td><td>○</td><td>• fans from all races, countries</td></tr>
<tr><td>conclusion</td><td></td><td>Conc: Rap brings people together; powerful like rock</td></tr>
</table>

Reviewing the Lecture

See the General Teaching Tips, page 12, for suggestions on teaching this section.

C. REAL TALK: USE WHAT YOU'VE LEARNED (page 98)

See the General Teaching Tips, page 13, for suggestions on teaching this section.

Vocabulary Review: Interview

See the General Teaching Tips, page 8, for suggestions on teaching this section.

SUGGESTED PROCEDURES

1. Go over the questions in the chart to ensure comprehension. For the last question, give examples of well-known performers who have openly expressed their political ideas (for example, Bono of U2, Bruce Springsteen).

2. Have students answer the questions about themselves in class or at home. They may wish to share these answers in class before the next step.

3. Have students gather information from their parents or someone of their parents' generation. Since these interviews will probably be conducted in their native language, have students translate the main points and write their notes in the chart in English.

4. In class, have students discuss ways in which their answers resembled or differed from another generation's. Monitor students to ensure that the lecture vocabulary gets used in the discussion.

Oral Report

Some of the students may have already done an oral presentation on this genre of music in the Oral Presentation exercise in Part One (see page 80 of the Student Book). Therefore, you can make this activity a voluntary one for extra credit. Encourage students not to choose lyrics that are offensive and to explain or translate the lyrics of the rap song they bring to class.

Part One: In Person

Background

The title of the chapter includes the common expression "getting (or to get) the job done," which simply means to finish a task or assignment, for example, "We can't go home until we get this job done."

Art

1. See the General Teaching Tips, page 3, for suggestions on presenting art.
2. The graph on page 100 shows the results of a survey in which 2,500 people were asked how satisfied they were with their jobs. The questions targeted factors such as pay, workload, hours, and advancement opportunities.

A. PRELISTENING (page 100)

Discussion

1. See the General Teaching Tips, page 3, for suggestions on conducting prelistening speaking activities.
2. If your students have never had a job, you can ask them to describe the positive and negative aspects of their parents' jobs or the job they plan to get when they finish studying. For fun, you could also ask them to describe the worst job they can imagine. What would make a job intolerable: the nature of the work, a horrible boss, low pay, long hours?

Vocabulary Preview

See the General Teaching Tips, page 4, for suggestions on conducting the vocabulary preview.

ANSWERS

1. e	3. f	5. g	7. j	9. h
2. a	4. d	6. c	8. i	10. b

B. LISTENING (page 102)

Main Ideas

See the General Teaching Tips, page 4, for suggestions on teaching the Main Ideas section.

① Answers

	Bonnie	Mike
Job	promoting yogurt	night janitor in old people's home
Responsibilities	handing people samples of yogurt to try	clean/scrub toilets
Why it was a bad job	it made runners sick. The bottoms fell out of the packaging and the yogurt spilled on people's clothes.	had to work at night, depressing, felt weird, set apart from the rest of the world

Details and Inferences

1. See the General Teaching Tips, page 5, for suggestions on teaching this section.
2. If this activity is difficult, play the recording section by section. Pause the recording after the answer to each question. Ask students: *What did you just hear? So what is the answer? How do you know?* This will train them to listen for context clues.

② Answers

Question	Clues
1. b. False	She says she used to hate yogurt.
2. b	Bonnie says they ate it quickly, they "threw it back" after running 26 miles.
3. b	Bonnie says the bottoms fell out of the packaging because it had not been perfected.
4. c	Bonnie says the yogurt went all over people's outfits.
5. b	It was an old people's home.
6. b. False	There were no other workers in the building, but the residents of the building—the old people—were there.
7. b	Mike came to work at 5 p.m. and left at 4 a.m. Vampires, according to legend, only come out at night.
8. c	He says he felt "set apart from the whole rest of the world."
9. c	He says he was making "pretty good money."

Listening for Language

See the General Teaching Tips, page 5, for suggestions on teaching this section.

FOCUS ON SOUND

1. See the General Teaching Tips, page 5, for suggestions on teaching Focus on Sound.
2. Rising intonation at the end of a phrase or sentence, also called *upspeak* or *uptalk,* has become more common in recent years in certain regions of the United States. In southern California, for example, it is a distinctive feature of the speech of many teenage girls.

④ ANSWERS

1. falling	**5.** falling	**9.** falling	**13.** rising
2. rising	**6.** falling	**10.** rising	**14.** falling
3. falling	**7.** falling	**11.** rising	**15.** falling
4. rising	**8.** rising	**12.** falling	

CONVERSATION TOOLS

See the General Teaching Tips, page 6, for suggestions on teaching Conversation Tools.

⑧ ANSWERS

1. Are you serious? (rising)

2. Oh my gosh! (falling)

3. Oh no! (falling)

C. REAL TALK: USE WHAT YOU'VE LEARNED (page 106)
Vocabulary Review: Questions and Answers

1. See the General Teaching Tips, page 6, for suggestions on conducting the vocabulary review.
2. To prevent students from reading their partners' questions, only the student asking the questions should have his or her book open. The listener's book should be closed.

Oral Presentation

1. See the General Teaching Tips, page 7, for suggestions on conducting discussions.
2. Students should do Exercise 1 independently, then form groups for Exercise 2.

Part Two: On the Phone

Art

1. See the General Teaching Tips, page 3, for suggestions on presenting art.
2. A handshake is customary when people are meeting for the first time in a business context.

A. PRELISTENING (PAGE 108)

Discussion

1. See the General Teaching Tips, page 3, for suggestions on conducting prelistening speaking activities.
2. There is some variation in the way people search for jobs, but the order given below is quite common. An applicant would call a company to find out if the job is still available and to request an application. The person would then send in a résumé and wait for an invitation to come in for an interview (which may or may not come!). After the interview, the applicant would follow up with a simple thank-you note to the interviewer.

ANSWERS

The usual order of activities is:
- **(1)** find out about the job
- **(2)** call a company
- **(3)** send in a résumé
- **(4)** make an appointment for an interview
- **(5)** go for an interview
- **(6)** follow up
- **(7)** wait for an answer

Vocabulary Preview

See the General Teaching Tips, page 4, for suggestions on conducting the vocabulary preview.

ANSWERS

1. h	**4.** a	**7.** c	**10.** f
2. k	**5.** b	**8.** d	**11.** g
3. j	**6.** i	**9.** e	

B. LISTENING (page 109)

Main Ideas

1. See the General Teaching Tips, page 4, for suggestions on teaching the Main Ideas section.
2. *Note:* In the recording, the applicant mentions that he worked at the "Study Abroad department" at the university. Many American universities offer students the opportunity to spend one or two semesters studying in another country, most often in their third (junior) year of college.

ANSWERS

1. He wants to follow up on his job application.
2. She wants to know about his international experience—whether he has worked with an international clientele. She also asks about his responsibilities when he worked in the Study Abroad department at the university.
3. Scott will come in for an interview.

Details and Inferences

See the General Teaching Tips, page 5, for suggestions on teaching this section.

❷ ANSWERS

1. F
2. F
3. F (The recording gives no information about why he quit.)
4. T
5. T

Listening for Language

See the General Teaching Tips, page 5, for suggestions on teaching this section.

FOCUS ON SOUND

See the General Teaching Tips, page 5, for suggestions on teaching Focus on Sound.

❹ ANSWERS

1. hesitant
2. hesitant
3. certain
4. certain
5. hesitant

C. REAL TALK: USE WHAT YOU'VE LEARNED (page 111)

Vocabulary Review: Discussion

See the General Teaching Tips, page 6, for suggestions on conducting the vocabulary review. See page 7 for suggestions on conducting post-listening discussions.

Role Play

1. See the General Teaching Tips, page 7, for suggestions on conducting role plays.
2. To make this activity more challenging and more authentic, instruct students not to look at their partners' information.

Problem Solving

The following items on the Job Application Form are illegal in the United States:
How long at this address?
Age, Height, Weight
Marital status, Number of children, Their ages
Religious Holidays Observed
Reason for leaving previous job
All the "Other" questions

Part Three: On the Air

Background

The listening segment in this part is from a radio program called *Marketplace*. The host interviews Peter Post and his wife, Peggy, who run the Emily Post Institute, named after Peter's grandmother Emily Post (died 1960). In her day Emily Post was the foremost expert on manners and etiquette in America.

Art

See the General Teaching Tips, page 3, for suggestions on presenting art.

A. PRELISTENING (page 114)
Discussion

1. See the General Teaching Tips, page 3, for suggestions on conducting prelistening speaking activities.
2. In the first sketch, the man using the copier is being rude. The woman has only one page to copy, so he should let her go first. In the second picture, the woman on the phone is talking loudly and disturbing her coworker.

Vocabulary Preview

See the General Teaching Tips, page 4, for suggestions on conducting the vocabulary preview.

ANSWERS

1. i	**4.** k	**7.** j	**10.** g
2. f	**5.** b	**8.** d	**11.** h
3. a	**6.** c	**9.** e	

B. LISTENING (page 115)
Main Ideas

See the General Teaching Tips, page 4, for suggestions on teaching the Main Ideas section.

❶ ANSWERS

1. using a speaker phone
2. forwarding e-mail
3. leaving your job
4. a boss receiving an unexpected resignation letter

Details and Inferences

See the General Teaching Tips, page 5, for suggestions on teaching this section.

❷ ANSWERS

Advice on Proper Etiquette	
1.	• Ask the other person, . . . "Do you mind if I use the speaker phone?" • Identify the other people in the room.
2.	Don't put anything private in an e-mail.
3.	Don't leave mad. Be professional. Don't burn bridges.
4.	The boss should . . . wish the person well and thank the person for his/her work

Listening for Language

See the General Teaching Tips, page 5, for suggestions on teaching this section.

CONVERSATION TOOLS

1. See the General Teaching Tips, page 6, for suggestions on teaching Conversation Tools.
2. "Do you mind" and "Would you mind' may require some additional explanation. Students may have difficulty understanding that "No, I don't mind" is a way of granting permission. Explain that "I don't mind" means "I have no objection" or "It doesn't bother me." In contrast, the responses "Yes, I do mind" and "Yes, it would bother me" indicate that the speaker strongly objects to the speaker's request, for example:

   Speaker 1: Do you mind if I smoke here?
   Speaker 2: Yes, I do mind. Please smoke outside.

C. REAL TALK: USE WHAT YOU'VE LEARNED (page 117)

Vocabulary Review: Discussion

1. See the General Teaching Tips, page 6, for suggestions on teaching this section.
2. The following words from the Vocabulary Preview are not covered in the review activity. You may want to ask students to form their own sentences with these words:
   repress
   poised

Survey

1. See the General Teaching Tips, page 8, for suggestions on conducting surveys and interviews.
2. If students are unable to speak with English speakers, they could interview friends, relatives, or acquaintances using their native language and record the answers in the chart in English.

Part Four: In Class

A. PRELISTENING (page 119)

See the General Teaching Tips, page 9, for suggestions on conducting prelistening activities in this part of the chapter.

Discussion

Students should notice that Americans and people in Asian countries tend to work more hours per year than Europeans. They should also notice that American law doesn't provide workers with any paid vacation days. Vacation is provided at the discretion of one's employer and written into one's job contract.

Vocabulary Preview

See the General Teaching Tips, page 4, for suggestions on conducting the vocabulary preview.

ANSWERS

1. g	**4.** h	**7.** c
2. e	**5.** i	**8.** d
3. f	**6.** a	**9.** b

B. LISTENING AND NOTE-TAKING (page 121)

Lecture Organization: Cause and Effect

See the General Teaching Tips, page 10, for suggestions on teaching this section.

❷ ANSWER

causes

Lecture Language: Cause and Effect

See the General Teaching Tips, page 1, for suggestions on teaching this section.

❹ ANSWERS

1. do you explain
2. the main reason
3. because, lead to
4. so
5. causes

Taking Notes

See the General Teaching Tips, page 11, for suggestions on teaching this section.

topic	Why Amer. work hard?
intro	–Amer. work as many hrs. as Jap. + Kor.
	– " " 300–400 hrs./yr. > than West. Euro
	– take fewer vacations
	– retire later
	Reasons
	1. Historical: Euros. who settled U.S. = relig. Christians
	believed in value of hard work
	that value → until today
	2. Main reason: economic
	U.S.: wide range of sal.
	e.g.: Pres. of U.S. co. earns 50–100 x av. wkr. →
	incentives to work harder, i.e., work hard → higher pay
	Europe: wage gap smaller → less incentive
	3. To keep job w/ benefits
	benefits = med. insurance, unemp. ins., retirement
	Europe: gov. pays ben.
	U.S.: employer pays ben. if lose job → lose ben.
	4. Technology → people work harder
	– how? e-mail, voicemail, etc. → easier to stay in
	touch w/ office
	– good jobs hard to find → people feel pressured
positive reason	5. They enjoy working
	work gives identity + sense of accomplishment
	feel part of team = Amer. value
	work gives reward > money
summary	People work hard for reward, or out of necessity

Reviewing the Lecture

1. See the General Teaching Tips, page 12, for suggestions on teaching this section.
2. Give students a copy of the Audioscript, if you choose.

C. REAL TALK: USE WHAT YOU'VE LEARNED (page 125)

See the General Teaching Tips, page 13, for suggestions on teaching this section.

Vocabulary Review: Discussion

See the General Teaching Tips, page 6, for suggestions on teaching this section.

Problem Solving

1. Read, or have a student read, the directions. Have students form groups of either three or five (odd numbers). Give students a time limit.
2. Go over the expressions in the Conversation Tools box. Model the pronunciation.
3. The challenge in this activity is that students need to agree on which worker to fire. If they can't come to an agreement, students within the group should vote and the majority should decide.
4. At the end, have each group share its decision.
5. If you wish to extend the activity, tell students that it has become necessary to lay off another worker, and have them discuss which worker they would lay off next.

CHAPTER 6 — TO YOUR HEALTH!

Part One: In Person

Art

See the General Teaching Tips, page 3, for suggestions on presenting art.

A. PRELISTENING (page 128)

Discussion

1. See the General Teaching Tips, page 3, for suggestions on conducting prelistening speaking activities.
2. Most students will probably be able to respond to the first question by using some form of the word *allergy*. You may want to quickly review the various ways to use this word:

   to have an allergy / allergies
   to be allergic (to something)

   You may also want to explain the difference between the words *cure* and *treat* as students often misuse these terms.

Vocabulary Preview

See the General Teaching Tips, page 4, for suggestions on conducting the vocabulary preview.

ANSWERS

1. e	**3.** f	**5.** h	**7.** d
2. a	**4.** c	**6.** g	**8.** b

B. LISTENING (page 130)

Main Ideas

See the General Teaching Tips, page 4, for suggestions on teaching the Main Ideas section.

🔘 ANSWERS
1. Lisa had to get rid of her cat.
2. She is allergic to cats (and other things like dust, pollen, mold).
3. felt lethargic, didn't have energy, was sneezing a lot, eyes were itchy and irritated, had headaches
4. pills, nasal spray
5. no

Details and Inferences

See the General Teaching Tips, page 5, for suggestions on teaching this section.

② **ANSWERS**

   a. three months

   b. a couple of (2) weeks

   c. dust, mold, pollen

   d. sleepy

③ **ANSWERS**

   a. F (She thought she just had a cold, so she didn't go to the doctor at first.)

   b. T

   c. F (She said she "had been around cats.")

   d T

   e. T

④ **ANSWERS**

   a. worried

   b. sympathetic, concerned, surprised

Listening for Language

See the General Teaching Tips, page 5, for suggestions on teaching this section.

FOCUS ON SOUND

See the General Teaching Tips, page 5, for suggestions on teaching Focus on Sound.

⑥ **ANSWERS**

   2. I'm just pretty bummed out. / I <u>had</u> to get <u>rid</u> / of my <u>cat</u>.

   3. I actually found <u>out</u> / that I was <u>allergic</u>.

   4. About <u>three</u> months ago / I started feeling pretty <u>out</u> of it.

   5. I had just <u>gotten</u> the <u>cat</u> / probably a couple of weeks <u>before</u>.

⑦ **ANSWERS**

   1. And <u>so</u> / you went to a <u>doctor</u>, or . . . / how did you find <u>out</u> / whether, what were your <u>symptoms</u>?

   2. Um, yeah, / so I <u>started</u>, / I was just feeling really <u>lethargic</u>, / and I didn't have any <u>energy</u>, / and you know / I was <u>sneezing</u> a lot, / and my eyes were really <u>itchy</u> and <u>irritated</u>, / and I had <u>headaches</u>.

   3. Well at <u>first</u> / I just <u>thought</u> / I was coming <u>down</u> / with a <u>cold</u>.

   4. Well I had <u>told</u> him that I had, / you know, / when I <u>thought</u> about it / after a <u>while</u> / when I couldn't figure <u>out</u>, / you know, / what <u>possibly</u> could be <u>wrong</u>, / after I knew it wasn't just a <u>cold</u>, / and I was like / "Oh, I just got this <u>cat</u> / not long <u>before</u>." /

   5. And so / the doctor <u>said</u>, / "You know, / well, we should run some <u>tests</u> / to see if you're <u>allergic</u>."

CONVERSATION TOOLS

See the General Teaching Tips, page 6, for suggestions on teaching Conversation Tools.

⑨ ANSWERS

Possible answers include the following:

    1. What a bummer. / That's too bad.

    2. I'm so sorry to hear that. / That's awful/terrible.

    3. I'm so sorry to hear that. / That's awful/terrible. / What a shame.

    4. That's too bad. / What a bummer.

    5. I'm (so, very) sorry to hear that. / My condolences.

    6. That's too bad.

C. REAL TALK: USE WHAT YOU'VE LEARNED (page 133)

Vocabulary Review: Discussion

    1. See the General Teaching Tips, page 6, for suggestions on conducting the vocabulary review.

    2. As students discuss various illnesses or medical conditions, be prepared to supply the necessary vocabulary for these conditions. (*Illness* implies a temporary sickness such as the flu. A *medical condition* refers to something chronic like diabetes, and/or ongoing such as back pain.) If some students don't feel comfortable discussing their health, encourage them to talk about someone they know or have known with an illness.

Role Play

See the General Teaching Tips, page 7, for suggestions on conducting the role play.

Part Two: On the Phone

A. PRELISTENING (page 135)

Discussion

See the General Teaching Tips, page 3, for suggestions on conducting prelistening speaking activities.

SAMPLE ANSWERS

- The purpose of the medication is to relieve symptoms (runny nose, sneezing, itchy/watery eyes) of allergies or a cold.
- It's used for allergies or a cold.
- If you exceed the recommended dosage, you could experience excitability or drowsiness.
- This medicine shouldn't be used by children under age 6.

Vocabulary Preview

See the General Teaching Tips, page 4, for suggestions on conducting the vocabulary preview.

ANSWERS

1. g	3. d	5. b	7. f
2. a	4. c	6. e	

B. LISTENING (page 136)

Main Ideas

See the General Teaching Tips, page 4, for suggestions on teaching the Main Ideas section.

❶ ANSWERS
1. a woman who is having trouble falling asleep
2. to find out if it is OK to take Benesec
3. ✓ It is used mainly for allergies.
   ✓ It is an antihistamine.
   ✓ Drowsiness is a side effect.
   ✓ It is safer than plants or herbs.

Details and Inferences

See the General Teaching Tips, page 5, for suggestions on teaching this section.

❷ ANSWERS
1. c
2. dryness ("It might dry you out.")
3. He is concerned that the woman is having difficulty sleeping every night.
4. She needs to find out the cause of the sleeping problem.
5. a

Listening for Language

See the General Teaching Tips, page 5, for suggestions on teaching this section.

CONVERSATION TOOLS

See the General Teaching Tips, page 6, for suggestions on teaching Conversation Tools.

❹ ANSWERS
1. I'm worried
   there's no need to worry
2. Don't get excited, Dad
3. I'm really scared
   I wouldn't worry if I were you
4. I'm not real comfortable
   I'm sure it's nothing serious

C. REAL TALK: USE WHAT YOU'VE LEARNED (page 139)

Vocabulary Review: Discussion

1. See the General Teaching Tips, page 6, for suggestions on conducting the vocabulary review.
2. *Note:* In the United States, many popular magazines contain advertisements for medication. If such ads are not available in the area where you teach, ask students to bring over-the-counter medication from home. As an alternative, you may want to bring in medicine bottles that you feel comfortable showing the students.

Part Three: On the Air

A. PRELISTENING (page 140)

Discussion

See the General Teaching Tips, page 3, for suggestions on conducting prelistening speaking activities.

SAMPLE ANSWERS

* The woman in the short skirt looks slim, thin, skinny, healthy.
* The couple looks heavy, overweight, obese.
* The overweight couple might develop heart disease or diabetes.
* Obesity is the condition of being very overweight.

Vocabulary Preview

See the General Teaching Tips, page 4, for suggestions on conducting the vocabulary preview.

ANSWERS

1. f	**3.** a	**5.** d
2. c	**4.** b	**6.** e

B. LISTENING (page 142)

Main Ideas

See the General Teaching Tips, page 4, for suggestions on teaching the Main Ideas section.

ANSWERS
1. c
2. a, b, e, f, g

Details and Inferences

See the General Teaching Tips, page 5, for suggestions on teaching this section.

❸ ANSWERS

	United States	World
Statistics	• 2/3 adults (127 mill) overweight • 30% (60 mill) _____ obese • 9 mill _____ severely obese	• Obese adults: 200 mill _____ ➤ 300 million from 1995 to 2000
Causes	• Huge variety of inexpensive food • High fat / energy dense foods in huge portions	• Diet becomes Americanized ➤ more fat • 17.5 mill children overweight

❹ SAMPLE ANSWERS

For Exercise 4, monitor students to make sure they produce complete sentences, using appropriate prepositions and subject-verb agreement. Do not require students to reproduce the information exactly as it appeared in the radio report; rather, the aim is to have students reconstruct their notes into accurate and complete sentences of their own.

- Two-thirds of adults are overweight in the United States. / 127 million Americans are overweight.
- Thirty percent of Americans are obese.
- Nine million adults in the United States are severely obese.
- The number of obese adults around the world increased from 200 million to 300 million from 1995 to 2000.
- There are 17.5 million obese children around the world.
- Americans are overweight because of the huge variety of inexpensive, high-fat, energy-dense foods. One cause of obesity in the United States is the huge portions that people eat.
- Diets around the world are becoming Americanized, which results in more fat consumption

Listening for Language

See the General Teaching Tips, page 5, for suggestions on teaching this section.

❻ ANSWERS

1. Doctors, report
2. According to scientists
3. Medical researchers found
4. says a report, British government
5. A study, suggests

❼ SAMPLE ANSWERS

Student A
- According to the World Health Organization, France and Italy have the best overall health care systems.

- Authorities in India reported (found) 1,600 cases of polio in the year 2000.
- The National Women's Health Information Center says that one-fifth of American women smoke.

Student B
- The Rand Corporation claims that health care spending by obese Americans is 36 percent higher than by normal-weight Americans. / Obese Americans spend 36 percent more on health care than normal-weight Americans do, according to the Rand Corporation.
- The Thai government says the bird flu epidemic is over.
- A study in China suggests that tea drinkers are as likely to develop cancer as non–tea drinkers are.

C. REAL TALK: USE WHAT YOU'VE LEARNED (page 144)

Vocabulary Review: Discussion

See the General Teaching Tips, page 6, for suggestions on conducting the vocabulary review.

SAMPLE ANSWERS

1. Diets around the world are becoming more Americanized due to the growing presence of American fast-food companies in other countries.
2. Obesity and being overweight might be a sign (symptom) of emotional problems such as insecurity, feelings of rejection, or lack of self-worth. Obesity and being overweight might also *result in* these psychological problems.
3. Being heavy is more accepted by some cultures than others. American society both accommodates and rejects overweight people. For example, many department stores sell extra-large clothes to accommodate overweight shoppers. On the other hand, many overweight people suffer from discrimination in the workplace, although such discrimination is prohibited by law.
4. The information below summarizes some of the trends indicated in the graph. Although students should be able to notice some of these trends, you may want to share this information with them following the *class* discussion:

In poor communities people tend to get fatter as their *incomes* rise, while in developed and transitional economies, higher income correlates with slimmer shapes.

Studies on the relationship between poverty and being overweight have identified a number of socioeconomic factors at work. Some have linked low stature and growth stunting due to fetal and early malnutrition with obesity in later life. Cultural factors are also important: many minority and lower income groups associate fatness with prosperity.

Gender differences further complicate the picture. In general, women tend to have higher rates of obesity than men. But rates of overweight are higher for men than women in developed countries yet higher for women than men in developing ones. Moreover, in many developing countries, the relationship between socioeconomic status and obesity is positive for men but negative for women.

Source: Adapted from *Perspectives in Health Magazine,* Volume 7, Number 3, 2002.

Art

See the General Teaching Tips, page 3, for suggestions on presenting art.

A. PRELISTENING (page 145)

Discussion

See the General Teaching Tips, page 9, for suggestions on conducting prelistening speaking activities.

QUIZ: *OBESITY AND WEIGHT LOSS*

The purpose of this quiz is not to test but to activate the students' prior knowledge about dieting and obesity. Encourage students to guess the answers if they are not familiar with this topic.

SUGGESTED PROCEDURES
1. Have students answer the questions individually in class or at home.
2. Have students compare their answers in groups *before* checking the answers on page 152 of the Student Book. Encourage students to discuss differences between their answers and the reasons for their choices.
3. Have students check the answers and discuss any surprising information.

Vocabulary Preview

See the General Teaching Tips, page 4, for suggestions on conducting the vocabulary preview.

ANSWERS

1. c	**3.** a	**5.** h	**7.** f
2. d	**4.** g	**6.** e	**8.** b

B. LISTENING AND NOTE-TAKING (page 148)

Lecture Language: Expressions of Comparison and Contrast

See the General Teaching Tips, page 11, for suggestions on teaching this section.

❷ ANSWERS

(Student responses will vary.)
1. Fish is high in protein. Similarly, chicken is a high-protein food.
   Most vegetarians don't eat chicken, while fish is part of the diet of many vegetarians.
2. Jogging and yoga are alike: They are both popular forms of exercise these days.
   Jogging can be very hard on the knees. Yoga, on the other hand, doesn't put any stress on the knees or other joints.

3. Bananas are nutritious. Similarly, an apple contains important vitamins and minerals.
Bananas are high in potassium. In contrast, apples are high in vitamin C. Bananas are
not high in protein. They are high in potassium.

4. A sore throat is a symptom of a cold. Likewise, a runny nose indicates a cold.
A runny nose is uncomfortable but not painful. A sore throat, however, can be very
painful.

5. Just like sleep, exercise is an important part of a healthy lifestyle.
While sleep is essential for survival, exercise is not.

6. Ice cream resembles steak in that they both contain a lot of fat.
Unlike steak, ice cream contains both fat and sugar.

Lecture Organization: Comparison and Contrast

See the General Teaching Tips, page 10, for suggestions on teaching this section.

❸ PROCEDURES

1. Have students describe the differences between the two sets of notes.
Block organization: The two contrasted topics (Coca-Cola and coffee) are described
separately. The two topics being contrasted are discussed in separate blocks or paragraphs. For example, all the information about Coca-Cola is presented in one para-
graph, and all the contrasting information about coffee is presented in the next.

Point-by-point organization: Information is organized according to a set of characteristics (points), such as flavor, sweetness, price, and the topics being contrasted
(coffee and Coca-Cola) are discussed alternately under each point.

2. Find out which organization type students prefer.

Taking Notes

See the General Teaching Tips, page 11, for suggestions on teaching this section.

❹ SAMPLE OUTLINE

intro	Q to nutritionist: Most effective diet?
	Answ: # of overweight people ↑, → many kinds of diets
◯	(most = fads)
	2 common diets: low-fat, low-carb
first type of diet	A. Low-fat diet
description	1. limit fat, oils (no meat, cheese, butter, fried foods)
advantage	2. adv: low cholesterol → no ♥ disease
problems	3. disadv: bored, hungry → overeat sugary foods →
	gain back weight

(continued)

second diet		B. Low-Carb diet
differences	◯	1. fat OK but cut down on carbs (sweets, bread, rice, potatoes); Atkins: no fruit
advantages		2. adv: lose weight
problems		3. disadv: bad for body (vitamin defic., kidney problems)
		e.g., Atkins = too extreme
similarities of two diets		C. Both limit food choice → hard to continue → gain weight back
conclusion	◯	D. Advice
		1. eat balanced diet (all food grps)
		2. reduce calories (smaller portions)
		3. exercise

Reviewing the Lecture

See the General Teaching Tips, page 12, for suggestions on teaching this section.

⑤ ANSWERS

1. block organization
2. Similarities: Both limit food choices; both are difficult to stay on; people on both diets often cheat and gain the weight back.
   Differences: Low-fat diet doesn't allow much fat. Low-carb diet allows fat but not carbohydrates.
3. First reason: People get frustrated eating only certain kinds of allowed food; as a result, they go off the diet.
   Second reason: People get hungry and overeat the foods they *are* allowed to eat.
4. Neither one.
5. Eat a balanced diet, reduce portions, and exercise regularly.

C. REAL TALK: USE WHAT YOU'VE LEARNED (page 151)

Vocabulary Review: Discussion

See the General Teaching Tips, page 6, for suggestions on conducting the vocabulary review.

Oral Report

SUGGESTED PROCEDURES
1. Allow students adequate time to prepare their presentations at home.
2. Provide guidelines for both the speaker and the audience. For example, prepare an evaluation form such as the one following that students can fill out in order to give feedback to the speaker.

PEER EVALUATION SHEET

NAME OF SPEAKER _____

TOPIC _____ DATE _____

	Excellent	Good	Fair	Poor
Organization				
Clarity (loudness, pronunciation, speed)				
Body language (eye contact, gestures, movement)				
Interest for you				
Use of media (handouts, computers, etc.)				
Overall grade				

Main point of presentation:

_____

_____

Two questions to ask this speaker:

_____

_____

Comments or suggestions for this speaker:

_____

_____

_____

CHAPTER 7

SHOP 'TIL YOU DROP

Part One: In Person

Background

See the Culture Note on page 154 of the Student Book.

The title "Shop 'til you drop" is an idiom. It is used when someone likes to shop and does so for enjoyments, and not out of necessity.

Art

See the General Teaching Tips, page 3, for suggestions on presenting art.

A. PRELISTENING (page 153)

Discussion

1. See the General Teaching Tips, page 3, for suggestions on conducting prelistening speaking activities.
2. Read the Culture Note, page 154, with students before dividing them into groups for the discussion. Ask a student or two to tell about a time they returned something to a store.

Vocabulary Preview

See the General Teaching Tips, page 4, for suggestions on conducting the vocabulary preview.

ANSWERS

1. d	**3.** h	**5.** a	**7.** f
2. b	**4.** g	**6.** e	**8.** c

B. LISTENING (page 155)

Main Ideas

1. See the General Teaching Tips, page 4, for suggestions on teaching the Main Ideas section.
2. Play the conversations separately. Have students answer the questions for the first conversation before they hear the second one.

❶ ANSWERS
  1. The zipper broke on her jacket and she wants to return it and get her money back.
  2. No refunds on sale merchandise.
  3. The salesclerk is going to get the manager so that the customer can talk to her.

❷ ANSWERS
  1. The customer and the store manager.
  2. No.

Details and Inferences

See the General Teaching Tips, page 5, for suggestions on teaching this section.

③ ANSWERS

1. there aren't any more.	**4.** T	**7.** T
2. T	**5.** T	**8.** T
3. T	**6.** F	**9.** b

Listening for Language

See the General Teaching Tips, page 5, for suggestions on teaching this section.

FOCUS ON SOUND

1. See the General Teaching Tips, page 5, for suggestions on teaching Focus on Sound.
2. Note about dropped /h/: In North American English, the dropped /h/ is most common with the pronouns *him, his, her.* (Pronouns are normally unstressed.) Notice that /h/ is not dropped in stressed words.

⑤ ANSWERS

1. Would you like to exchange the jacket for another one?
2. Did you want to get something else?
3. I'd like to just get my money back.
4. I'll get her for you.
5. I didn't know that when I bought the jacket or I never would have bought it.
6. Couldn't you give me a break just this once?

CONVERSATION TOOLS

See the General Teaching Tips, page 6, for suggestions on teaching this section.
In Exercise 8, have students look up (*not* read) while listening to their partner.

⑧ SUGGESTED ANSWERS

Student A

a. What a steal.

b. It's a rip-off. / It costs an arm and a leg. / You paid through the nose.

c. It's a good deal.

d. What a rip-off!

Student B

a. What a steal.

b. It's a good deal. / It's a bargain.

c. They cost a fortune.

d. It's a rip-off.

C. REAL TALK: USE WHAT YOU'VE LEARNED (page 158)

Vocabulary Review: Discussion

1. See the General Teaching Tips, page 6, for suggestions on conducting the vocabulary review. See page 7 for suggestions on conducting discussions.
2. Have students form original sentences with items that they don't use in the discussion, e.g., "headquarters."

Role Play

See the General Teaching Tips, page 7, for suggestions on conducting role plays.

Part Two: On the Phone

Art

See the General Teaching Tips, page 3, for suggestions on presenting art.

A. PRELISTENING (page 160)

Discussion

See the General Teaching Tips, page 3, for suggestions on conducting prelistening speaking activities.

ANSWERS
> *Sample questions to ask include:*
> What size cars do you have?
> What's the price for a sub-compact (compact, mid-size, luxury) car?
> How much does insurance cost?
> Where can I pick up the car? Where can I return it?
> How old do I have to be to rent a car?
> Can I rent a car with an international driver's license?

Vocabulary Preview

See the General Teaching Tips, page 4, for suggestions on conducting the vocabulary preview.

ANSWERS

1. i	**4.** h	**7.** d
2. g	**5.** b	**8.** e
3. a	**6.** c	**9.** f

B. LISTENING (page 162)

Main Ideas

1. See the General Teaching Tips, page 4, for suggestions on teaching the Main Ideas section.
2. Please note the instructions for conducting Exercises 1 and 2. The recording consists of phone calls to two different car rental companies. Therefore, the class is to be divided

into two groups. Each group hears one phone call and takes notes on the essential information. Afterward the two groups share information and decide on the best deal.

If it is impossible for you to divide your class into two groups, it is possible for all students to hear both phone conversations and answer all questions; however, this option will take away the information gap.

❶ ANSWERS

First call
1. to get information
2. the caller's relatives
3. She says thank you and hangs up. She does not rent a car.

Second call
1. to get information about rental rates
2. visitors from Italy
3. She says thank you and hangs up. She does not rent a car.

Details and Inferences

See the General Teaching Tips, page 5, for suggestions on teaching this section.

❸ ANSWERS

	Call 1	Call 2
	Best Deals Car Rental	**Discount Cars**
Daily rate	$39	$45 after first week
Weekly rate	$190	$249
Mileage	unlimited	unlimited
Insurance	not included	included
Tax		8.25% included
Foreign license	OK	
How many drivers allowed	3	
Age limit / surcharge	21	20 / $5 per day surcharge for under 25
Special package	Weekend special, Friday–Monday, unlimited mileage, $30 a day	Las Vegas Special, $119/three days, 600 free miles

Listening for Language

See the General Teaching Tips, page 5, for suggestions on teaching this section.

1. See the General Teaching Tips, page 5, for suggestions on teaching Focus on Sound.
2. In questions with falling intonation, the voice actually rises on the last stressed word before falling at the end, for example:

     What do you think about that?

🄢 **ANSWERS**

1. How can I help you?

2. May I help you?

3. When, uh, when did you need the car?

4. Do you know what size car?

5. The—what are the different options?

6. Would you like me to reserve one for you?

7. Oh, they do?

8. And is tax included, or is that extra, too?

9. And is that OK if they don't have a local driver's license?

10. What kind of car are you interested in?

11. How many people?

12. So are we looking at a mid-size car, a mini-van, or an SUV?

13. What about per day?

14. Is that your lowest rate?

15. What's your policy about drivers under twenty-one?

16. $5 extra per day?

C. REAL TALK: USE WHAT YOU'VE LEARNED (page 164)

Vocabulary Review: Conversation

See the General Teaching Tips, page 6, for suggestions on teaching this section.

ANSWERS

1. shop around	3. quoted	5. competitive	7. surcharge
2. promotional	4. valid	6. option	8. As long as

Information Gap

1. See the General Teaching Tips, page 9, for suggestions on conducting information gap activities.
2. An optional preliminary step is to put A students and B students in separate groups and have them work out the structure of the questions they will ask before doing the information gap activity.

Part Three: On the Air

Art

See the General Teaching Tips, page 3, for suggestions on presenting art.

A. PRELISTENING (page 166)

Discussion

See the General Teaching Tips, page 3, for suggestions on conducting prelistening speaking activities.

ANSWER
The man's problem is that there are too many choices, so he feels confused.

Vocabulary Preview

See the General Teaching Tips, page 4, for suggestions on conducting the vocabulary preview.

ANSWERS

1. g	**3.** a	**5.** c	**7.** f
2. e	**4.** b	**6.** d	

B. LISTENING (page 168)

Main Ideas

See the General Teaching Tips, page 4, for suggestions on teaching the Main Ideas section.

❶ ANSWERS

Satisfizers

Satisfied with "good enough"; have internal standards; don't worry about what other people are doing. When they find a product that meets their standards, they stop looking.

Maximizers

Must have the best; want to examine all the alternatives; plagued with doubt—they think if they'd gone to a different store, they could have found something better.

Details and Inferences

1. See the General Teaching Tips, page 5, for suggestions on teaching this section.
2. *Note:* Ronald Reagan was president of the United States from 1981 to 1989.

❷ ANSWERS

1. need to	**5.** don't care	**9.** good
2. impossible	**6.** what's good enough	**10.** agrees
3. doubt	**7.** don't worry	**11.** not better
4. have	**8.** less	

Listening for Language

See the General Teaching Tips, page 5, for suggestions on teaching this section.

❹ ANSWERS

1. to, digital	**3.** better	**5.** to	**7.** satisfied	**9.** matter
2. thirty, forty	**4.** get	**6.** what	**8.** alternatives	

❺ ANSWERS

Picture A

A note says: Party on Saturday; you're invited.

The test score is ninety-five.

The water bottle is open.

The clock shows a quarter to 9.

The child is sitting in a high-chair.

Picture B

A note has the babysitter's phone number.

The test score in ninety-nine.

There's a drawing of a kitty.

The child is patting the cat.

The water bottle is closed.

There is water in the glass.

C. REAL TALK: USE WHAT YOU'VE LEARNED (page 171)

Vocabulary Review: Discussion

1. See the General Teaching Tips, page 6, for suggestions on conducting the vocabulary review.
2. There are no correct answers to this "quiz."

Part Four: In Class

Art

See the General Teaching Tips, page 3, for suggestions on presenting art.

A. PRELISTENING (page 172)

See the General Teaching Tips, page 9, for suggestions on conducting prelistening speaking activities.

Discussion

1. See the General Teaching Tips, page 7, for suggestions on conducting discussions.
2. The photo is a scene from the television program *24*. The Apple computer is an example of product placement, which is a type of advertising.

Vocabulary Preview

See the General Teaching Tips, page 4, for suggestions on conducting the vocabulary preview.

ANSWERS

1. e   **2.** f   **3.** c   **4.** a   **5.** d   **6.** b

B. LISTENING AND NOTE-TAKING (page 174)

Lecture Language: Pro and Con Expressions

See the General Teaching Tips, page 11, for suggestions on teaching this section.

❷ ANSWERS

1. supporters

2. for / in favor of / in support of

3. against / opposed to

4. oppose

5. an opponent

❸ ANSWERS

1. two   **2.** one   **3.** On the other hand

Taking Notes

See the General Teaching Tips, page 11, for suggestions on teaching this section.
Before listening to the lecture, have students look at the photo and guess the brand of the car and the title of the movie it appeared in. (BMW Z8 driven by James Bond in the movie *The World Is Not Enough* will be mentioned in the lecture as an example of product placement.)

SAMPLE OUTLINE

		Topic: product placement
		ex: Apple computer in <u>24</u>
	◯	
definition		I. Def. of product placement
		• mentioning, using, showing a brand-name product as part of story
		• not commercial, but = type of advert.
		II. Media
		A. television
		ex: <u>Friends</u> - Ross eating Oreo cookie
		B. movies
		ex. James Bond - BMW, Coke/Pepsi

(continued)

```
┌─────────────────────────────────────────────────┐
│         │  C. video games                          │
│         ├──────────────────────────────────────────┤
│         │  D. pop songs                            │
│    ◯    ├──────────────────────────────────────────┤
│         │  E. books                                │
│         ├──────────────────────────────────────────┤
│         │    ex. candy in children's book          │
│         │                                          │
│  pro    │  III. Pro                                │
│         │    A. for advertisers: sells products    │
│         │       ex. candy sales, after movie ET, Tom Cruise │
│         │       + Ray Ban sunglasses               │
│         │    B. for consumers: makes stories realistic │
│         │                                          │
│  con    │  IV. Con                                 │
│         │    A. expose us to adv. against our will │
│         │    B. subtle → don't realize we're seeing adv. │
│         │    C. esp. true for children (Lancaster study) │
│    ◯    │                                          │
│conclusion│ Conc: Consumer groups want laws to restrict/ban prod. place. │
│         │  in media for kids                       │
│         │                                          │
└─────────────────────────────────────────────────┘
```

Reviewing the Lecture

See the General Teaching Tips, page 12, for suggestions on teaching this section.

C. REAL TALK: USE WHAT YOU'VE LEARNED (page 177)

See the General Teaching Tips, page 13, for suggestions on teaching this section.

Vocabulary Review: Discussion

See the General Teaching Tips, page 6, for suggestions on teaching this section.

Debate

1. Follow the steps in the Student Book for dividing students into groups, preparing, and presenting the debate.
2. Additional arguments in favor of product placement: It brings in money for advertisers; it is less intrusive than commercials.
3. Additional arguments against product placement: It is manipulative; it is a kind of brainwashing; it makes people, especially children, want things they don't need; it is distracting.

| **CHAPTER** **8** | DO THE RIGHT THING |

Part One: In Person

Art

See the General Teaching Tips, page 3, for suggestions on presenting art.

A. PRELISTENING (page 179)

Discussion

See the General Teaching Tips, page 3, for suggestions on conducting prelistening speaking activities.

Quiz: *What Is Cheating?*

The purpose of this quiz is to activate students' prior knowledge about the concept of cheating in the academic world. Encourage students to guess the answers if they are not familiar with this topic. Note that the correct answers are based on generally accepted rules of behavior in North American high schools and universities. These behaviors may or may not be considered appropriate in the cultures of the students you teach. Encourage students to discuss cross-cultural differences in what constitutes "cheating" and "plagiarism."

SUGGESTED PROCEDURES

1. Have students answer the questions individually in class or at home.
2. Have students compare their answers in groups *before* checking the answers on page 186 of the Student Book. Encourage students to discuss differences between their answers and the reasons for their choices.
3. Have students check the answers and discuss any surprising information.

Vocabulary Preview

See the General Teaching Tips, page 4, for suggestions on conducting the vocabulary preview.

ANSWERS

1. f	**3.** d	**5.** c
2. e	**4.** b	**6.** a

B. LISTENING (page 181)

Main Ideas

See the General Teaching Tips, page 4, for suggestions on teaching the Main Ideas section.

❶ ANSWERS

2, 4, 5

Details and Inferences

See the General Teaching Tips, page 5, for suggestions on teaching this section.

❷ ANSWERS

Speakers	Ways of Cheating	Would Cheat?	Would Be Tempted?
Male Student	1. not hand in all pages of paper, lie about it to gain more time	No	Yes (says "I might consider it.")
	2. send each other the correct answers through Instant Messenger during open laptop test		
Female Student 1	never hand in paper & lie that they did	Maybe	Yes
Female Student 2	copy answers from a straight-A student sitting next to you	Yes	Yes

Listening for Language

See the General Teaching Tips, page 5, for suggestions on teaching this section.

CONVERSATION TOOLS

See the General Teaching Tips, page 6, for suggestions on teaching Conversation Tools.

FOCUS ON SOUND

See the General Teaching Tips, page 5, for suggestions on teaching Focus on Sound.

❼ ANSWERS

1. would lie	**4.** would you steal	**7.** would your mom	**10.** wouldn't be
2. wouldn't do	**5.** would understand	**8.** would	
3. would you	**6.** wouldn't be	**9.** wouldn't they	

C. REAL TALK: USE WHAT YOU'VE LEARNED (page 184)

Vocabulary Review: Discussion

See the General Teaching Tips, page 7, for suggestions on conducting the discussion.

Take a Survey

See the General Teaching Tips, page 8, for suggestions on conducting surveys and interviews.

Part Two: On the Phone

Art

See the General Teaching Tips, page 3, for suggestions on presenting art.

A. PRELISTENING (page 188)

Discussion

1. See the General Teaching Tips, page 3, for suggestions on conducting prelistening speaking activities.
2. *Culture Note:* In North America, most public institutions as well as large stores maintain a "lost and found" department where found items are kept for a limited time. Small items found on public streets are rarely turned in to the police as they are in many other countries.
3. "Finders keepers, losers weepers": Originally a children's chant used by a child who found an object to the child who lost it to show that the finder intends to keep the item.

Vocabulary Preview

See the General Teaching Tips, page 4, for suggestions on conducting the vocabulary preview.

ANSWERS

1. f	**3.** g	**5.** c	**7.** d
2. a	**4.** e	**6.** b	

B. LISTENING (page 189)

Main Ideas

See the General Teaching Tips, page 4, for suggestions on teaching the Main Ideas section.

🔘 ANSWERS

The Recording
1. the university police "lost and found" department
2. leave a message
3. bring it to the police station

The Conversation
1. a staff member (an officer) of the university police lost and found department and a person who found a watch
2. a Rolex watch
3. reward

Details and Inferences

See the General Teaching Tips, page 5, for suggestions on teaching this section.

❷ ANSWERS

   1. F (They return calls only if they receive an item.)
   2. F (You must come to the station [the front desk] in person to check for sunglasses.)
   3. T
   4. T
   5. F (The caller can keep the watch if no one claims it after 90 days.)
   6. I (The caller says, "I'll think it over.")

Listening for Language

See the General Teaching Tips, page 5, for suggestions on teaching this section.

FOCUS ON SOUND

See the General Teaching Tips, page 5, for suggestions on teaching Focus on Sound.

❹ SAMPLE ANSWERS

A: Are you coming to work tomorrow?
B: No, I'm going to call in sick.

A: My friend is in the hospital. Should I ask her doctor how she is?
B: No. Doctors don't give out that kind of information to friends. They give it out only to family members.

A: What should I do with this wet umbrella? Leave it outside or bring it in?
B: Bring it in.

A: I need to mail this letter at the post office but I don't have time to go there today.
B: No problem; I can drop it off for you.

A: I just found a diamond ring in the bathroom of this restaurant.
B: You're going to turn it in to the manager, right?

A: I can't decide if I want to buy this car or not.
B: Why don't you think it over and let me know tomorrow.

CONVERSATION TOOLS

   1. See the General Teaching Tips, page 6, for suggestions on teaching Conversation Tools.
   2. This teaching segment may require a brief grammar review if students aren't familiar with the concept of *real* versus *unreal conditional.*

Student A

> Suppose your friend copied a term paper . . .
> What if your boyfriend lied to you . . .
> Let's say you were in love . . .
> What if you lost your passport . . .
> What if you didn't have a computer . . .

Student B

> What if your friend cheated on the final exam . . .
> Suppose you could speak six languages . . .
> Let's say you left your book bag on the bus . . .
> What if you saw your girlfriend drinking coffee with . . .
> What if you didn't have a job . . .

C. REAL TALK: USE WHAT YOU'VE LEARNED (page 192)

Vocabulary Review: Discussion

See the General Teaching Tips, page 6, for suggestions on conducting the vocabulary review.

Talk about It

1. For a detailed description of the experiment presented in this exercise, refer to the *Reader's Digest* Special Report "How Honest Are We?" by Ralph Kinney Bennett, December 1995, pp. 49–55.
2. You may want students to research and present the findings of the same experiment done by *Reader's Digest* in different countries in 2001. The results of this study showed the following percentages of returned wallets:

   Denmark—100%
   Norway—100%
   Singapore—90%
   Australia—70%
   Japan—70%
   U.S.—67%
   U.K.—65%
   Holland—50%
   Germany—45%
   Russia—43%
   Philippines—40%
   Italy—35%
   China—30%
   Mexico—21%

Source: http://www.usj.com.my/usjXpress/details.php3?table=usjXpress&ID=181

Part Three: On the Air

Art

See the General Teaching Tips, page 3, for suggestions on presenting art.

A. PRELISTENING (page 194)

See the General Teaching Tips, page 3, for suggestions on conducting prelistening speaking activities.

Discussion

1. See the General Teaching Tips, page 3, for suggestions on conducting prelistening speaking activities.
2. The news headline appears on the CBC (Canadian Broadcasting Corporation) website. The news report is about a research study on lying.

Vocabulary Preview

See the General Teaching Tips, page 4, for suggestions on conducting the vocabulary preview.

ANSWERS

1. e	**3.** f	**5.** b	**7.** d
2. g	**4.** a	**6.** c	

B. LISTENING (page 195)

Main Ideas

See the General Teaching Tips, page 4, for suggestions on teaching the Main Ideas section.

❶ ANSWERS

1. asked people to get to know another person and talk for 10 min.; the conversation was videotaped; people viewed videotape of their conversation; commented on "not accurate" info, i.e., lies
2. Sixty percent of the people lied at least once during the 10 minutes.

Details and Inferences

See the General Teaching Tips, page 5, for suggestions on teaching this section.

❷ ANSWERS

1. T
2. F (The average number of lies is 3.)
3. T
4. F (Men and women lie at about the same rate.)
5. T
6. T
7. I

Listening for Language

See the General Teaching Tips, page 5, for suggestions on teaching this section.

CONVERSATION TOOLS

See the General Teaching Tips, page 6, for suggestions on teaching Conversation Tools.

C. REAL TALK: USE WHAT YOU'VE LEARNED (page 197)
Vocabulary Review: Discussion

See the General Teaching Tips, page 6, for suggestions on conducting the vocabulary review.

Take a Survey

See the General Teaching Tips, page 8, for suggestions on conducting the survey.

Part Four: In Class

Art

See the General Teaching Tips, page 3, for suggestions on presenting art.

A. PRELISTENING (page 200)

See the General Teaching Tips, page 9, for suggestions on conducting prelistening speaking activities.

Discussion

See the General Teaching Tips, page 3, for suggestions on conducting speaking activities.

Vocabulary Preview

See the General Teaching Tips, page 4, for suggestions on conducting the vocabulary preview.

ANSWERS

1. e	**3.** a	**5.** b
2. d	**4.** f	**6.** c

B. LISTENING AND NOTE-TAKING (page 201)
Lecture Organization: Rhetorical Questions

See the General Teaching Tips, page 10, for suggestions on teaching this section.

1. to introduce a new topic (the choice between two actions that are both right)
2. to get the listener's attention

Lecture Language: Digressing

See the General Teaching Tips, page 11, for suggestions on teaching this section.

❹ **ANSWERS**

1. the self versus community dilemma
2. by the way
3. the movie *Erin Brockovich*
4. Anyway

Taking Notes

See the General Teaching Tips, page 11, for suggestions on teaching this section.

❺ **ANSWERS**

topic		Ethical dilemma: choice about right v. wrong behav.
		Topic: 3 types of right vs. right dilemmas:
1st type		1. Truth vs. loyalty
example		• e.g. friend using drugs - keep secret or tell?
example		• e.g. friend's dress unattractive/unprof.
		tell truth or keep quiet?
2nd type		2. Self vs. community
definition		• Def: needs of 1 person vs. needs of group/ community
example		• e.g. parents want you to be doctor; you want to be artist.
		whom to please?
example		• e.g. co. or gov. spilling dangerous chemicals; report them or not? protect your job or community?

(continued)

3rd type		3. Short term vs. Long term goals
example		• e.g. eat all candy now or save some for later (age 7)
example		• e.g. spend $ now on car or save $ for college (age 16)
example		• e.g. gov. keeps taxes low + be pop. or raises taxes for new univ. 5 yrs. later?
		Conflict: needs/desires of present vs. future
conclusion		Conc:
		• Ethical dilemmas not easy
		• Useful strategies/guidelines to help make right choices—next topic

Reviewing the Lecture

See the General Teaching Tips, page 12, for suggestions on teaching this segment.

Ⓖ Answers

1. three types of right versus right ethical dilemmas
2. see answer key for Exercise 5

C. REAL TALK: USE WHAT YOU'VE LEARNED (page 204)

Vocabulary Review: Discussion

1. See the General Teaching Tips, page 13, for suggestions on conducting the vocabulary review.
2. *Suggestion:* Have students review the list of Strategies for Resolving Ethical Dilemmas <u>before</u> discussing solutions to the problems in Exercise 2.

CHAPTER
TESTS

INTRODUCTION TO CHAPTER TESTS

Each chapter of **Real Talk 1** is accompanied by a test that measures how well students have mastered the vocabulary, conversational phrases, idioms, and phonological features presented in the chapter. Tests are worth 40 points each.

TEST FEATURES

* A variety of tasks (fill-in-the-blank, open-ended questions, matching, etc.)
* Answer keys and a scoring guide
* An Audioscript for the listening sections

SUGGESTIONS FOR USE

Since the tests cover all the material in the chapter, we recommend using the tests in their entirety only if you have taught all four parts of the chapter. Otherwise, feel free to customize the tests and use only parts that are appropriate for your class.

The listening portions of the tests are not recorded; therefore, we have provided scripts for the instructors to read. We have also included pronunciation guidelines for stress, reductions, linking, and intonation. We recommend reading the items once, at a natural speed, and adhering to the guidelines provided. You may also want to ask a native speaker to record these listening sections.

CHAPTER 1 TEST

A. Complete the sentences with a word or expression from the box. Change noun endings or verb forms if necessary. Not all words or expressions will be used. (10 points)

be sick of	go through with (something)	reputation
can't stand	hassle	tend to
differentiate	make sense	unconventional
explicit	medieval	unless

1. Yesterday I had $40 in my wallet. Today I have only $10. I didn't spend any money yesterday, so where did my money go? This doesn't _____.

2. Speakers of many languages are unable to _____ between the English /l/ and /r/ sounds.

3. We've eaten chicken every night this week. I _____ it. How about something different tonight, like spaghetti?

4. Don't lie. Once you get a _____ as a liar, it's almost impossible to change people's opinion of you.

5. I've noticed in language classes that people who speak the same first language _____ sit together.

6. Please turn off that horrible music! I _____ listening to it!

7. Driving downtown is a huge _____ because it's almost impossible to find parking.

8. _____ you start working on your project, you won't have enough time to finish it before the deadline.

9. My name is Shayne and my sister's name is Mackenzie. As you can see, my parents like _____ names.

10. The embassy staff received _____ instructions on the proper way to address foreign ambassadors and government ministers.

B. Complete the sentences with a word or expression from the box. Change noun endings or verb forms if necessary. Not all words or expressions will be used. (10 points)

address	linguist	statistics
estimate	loosen up	study (*noun*)
in authority	prospective	tendency
likely	reaction	title

1. At first the new students were shy, but after a couple of weeks they began to

    _____ and enjoy themselves in my class.

2. In some cultures, children should not make eye contact with a person

    _____, such as a teacher or police officer.

3. Do you think it's _____ that someday people will live on
   the planet Mars?

4. Karen Jalabi has been a reporter for more than 30 years. She can't even

    _____ how many people she has interviewed in all that time.

5. A recent _____ showed that children as young as seven can have
   high cholesterol levels.

6. My uncle was a _____ who spent his life studying the languages
   of Indonesia.

7. My economics teacher has a PhD, but he never uses the _____ "Dr."
   He always invites his students to use his first name.

8. What was your _____ when you heard that you had won first
   prize in the essay competition? Were you shocked?

9. The college invited all the _____ first-year students to an interview.

10. Don't believe everything Sue tells you. She has a _____ to exaggerate.

C. Write three true sentences about your name. In each sentence use at least one of the words or expressions from the box. Use a different word or expression in every sentence. (6 points)

ancestor	immediate family	named after (for)
call (*verb*)	middle name	nickname
family name	name (*verb*)	

1. _____

2. _____

3. _____

D. Your teacher will read the following sentences out loud. Underlined words are stressed. Listen and circle two more stressed words in each sentence. (10 points)

EXAMPLE:

I'm <u>sorry</u>, but I (can't) remember your (name.)

1. My brother is two <u>years</u> <u>younger</u> than <u>I</u> am.

2. The weather is <u>awful</u> today. I <u>wish</u> I could <u>stay</u> home.

3. Don't <u>sit</u> on the <u>chair</u> by the <u>window</u>. It's been broken since <u>last</u> <u>Sunday</u>.

4. Why are you leaving so <u>early</u>?

5. <u>Ming</u> couldn't <u>speak</u> <u>English</u> until he was <u>13 years</u> old.

E. Each item below has one error in the use of titles or names. Correct the errors. (4 points)

EXAMPLE:

Female teacher: Could you please open the window, Michael?
Young student: Yes, ~~sir~~. *ma'am*

1. **Customer:** This is Laura Hansen. I'm calling to get information about flights to London on June 19.

    Airline reservations agent: All right, Laura. Can I get some more information from you first?

2. **Man, age 60:** Could you bring me a glass of water, please?

    Waiter: Yes mister, right away.

3. **Married woman:** Hello?

    Friend of her son's: Hello, Miss Baker. This is Andrew. Can I speak to Charley?

    Woman: Sure, Andrew. I'll get him for you.

4. **Professor Smith:** Hello, Adam. How are you?

    Student: Hi, Smith. I'm fine, thank you.

CHAPTER 2 TEST

A. Complete the sentences with a word or expression from the box. Change noun endings or verb forms if necessary. Not all words or expressions will be used. (5 points)

anxiety	guideline	non-refundable	rate (*noun*)
at random	hazardous	outbreak	ripped off
book (*verb*)	intense	panic-stricken	show up
casualties	lack of	pay through the	stay over
deadline	lead to	nose	visibility
end up	messed up (*adj.*)	purchase	

1. To save money, try to buy your airline ticket at least three months before your trip.

If you wait too long, you will _____.

2. The professor announced that the _____ for turning in our papers was June 2, and he stressed that he would not accept late papers.

3. More than 20 people have died in the latest _____ of bird flu, according to today's newspaper.

4. David missed his flight because he arrived at the airport late, and then he was stopped

_____ for a security search.

5. We arrived in Venice, Italy, without a hotel reservation. Every cheap hotel in town was

booked. We _____ paying $300 a night to stay in a first-class hotel.

B. Write the word or expression from the box in part A that is the <u>opposite</u> of each of the numbered words below. (5 points)

1. calm (*adj.*)	
2. safe (*adj.*)	
3. sell	
4. disappear	
5. neat, orderly	

C. From the box in Part A, choose a synonym or definition for each word or expression in parentheses. Complete the sentence. Change noun endings or verb forms if necessary. (5 points)

1. The U.S. State Department has a website with lists of _____
   (suggestions)
   for people planning to travel abroad.

2. The furniture I bought six months ago is already falling apart. I feel really

   _____.
   (cheated)

3. Coffee _____ nervousness in some people and it should not be given
   (causes)
   to children.

4. There is a _____ food, clean water, and medicine in many parts
   (not enough)
   of Africa.

5. This hotel is too expensive in the summer, but the _____ goes down
   (cost)
   after September 1.

D. In the sentences below, arcs are used to connect linked words. Listen to the sentences and find one linking error in each. Circle it. (3 points)

EXAMPLE:

He's afraid to fly, so he ⟨travels by⟩ train or by bus.

1. The thing I can't stand about traveling is the small airplane seats. It's impossible to

   get comfortable.

2. The security officer told me to take all my things out of the suitcase.

3. Our plane couldn't land in London because of the thick fog and heavy rain.

E. Complete the following dialogues with expressions of irritation or annoyance. Use a different expression in each sentence. Do not use "can't stand." (6 points)

EXAMPLE:

A: This looks like a popular restaurant. Look at the long line of people at the door.

B: Yeah, but I _____*can't stand*_____ waiting in line. Let's eat somewhere else.

1. **A:** What's the matter, John? Aren't you enjoying the party?

   B: No. All the noise and people drinking _____.

2. **A:** _____ when Professor Baker gives us 300 pages to read
   in one week. Doesn't she know we have other classes, too?

   B: I know. Her class is really tough.

3. A: Do you hear that guy talking on his cell phone at the next table? It's so loud!

    B: You're right. That's rude. _____ when people do that.

F. Your friends tell you about their travel situations. Give them advice. Use a different expression in each sentence. (6 points)

  1. "My company is sending me to Tokyo on a business trip, but I don't know anything about Japan."

    Advice: _____

  2. "I'll need to leave town for three days. I don't know who can take care of my cat while I'm away."

    Advice: _____

  3. "I'm going to Spain in July. I heard that the weather is very hot then."

    Advice: _____

G. Write complete sentences containing the word and the definition. Use a different expression for defining terms in each sentence. (4 points)

Word	Definition
slang	nonstandard or informal language used by a particular group of people
sociology	the study of human beings as social animals

  1. _____

  2. _____

H. Answer the questions in complete sentences. (6 points)

  1. What is your travel pet peeve?

    _____

  2. What is a phobia?

    _____

  3. What is therapy?

    _____

A. Complete the story with a word or expression from the box. Change noun endings or verb forms if necessary. Not all words or expressions will be used. (10 points)

as far as	fall head over heels in love	pursue
associated with	match up	settle down
assume	on the basis of	wonder about
committed	passionate	

Jessica and Kevin are two young professionals from New York City. They were

_____ three years ago by Kevin's cousin, Mark. Mark
       1

_____ they would get along well _____ their personalities,
       2   3

and he was right. Both are outgoing, funny, and kind. _____ their interests
                                                    4

go, they have a lot in common also. For example, they are both _____ about
                                                            5

music and hiking.

Kevin and Jessica _____ after one date and they have been
                                    6

in a _____ relationship ever since. But even though they are very serious
       7

about each other, Jessica isn't sure she is ready to _____. She
                                                   8

_____ marriage and the responsibility of having children. She enjoys having
       9

the freedom to _____ new interests, travel, and meet new people. But since
           10

she and Kevin are both 30-something, she knows they will have to have a serious talk about

marriage in the near future.

B. For each word or expression in parentheses, choose a synonym or definition from the box and complete the sentence. Change noun endings or verb forms if necessary. Not all words or expressions will be used. (10 points)

ballpark figure	fulfilled	profile
chances are	keep in mind	solitude
drive	left out	stay out of it
dwindling	pool	

1. When a young couple argues, their parents should _____.
   (not interfere)

2. Derek and Tina have been dating for three years. _____ that they will get married.
   (It's likely)

3. Before you take her out to dinner, _____ that she is a vegetarian.
   (remember)

4. Hunger, thirst, and sexual desire are natural _____ of all human beings.
   (instinctive needs)

5. Mr. and Mrs. Jamison decided to get a divorce because neither one felt
   _____ by their relationship.
   (satisfied)

6. Come and join our conversation; we don't want you to feel
   _____.
   (that we don't want to include you)

7. Olivia enjoys reading the _____ on Internet dating websites, but she
   (descriptions of people)
   hasn't actually gone out with anyone she's read about yet.

8. My car needs a new transmission. Can you give me a _____ of what it
   (the approximate cost)
   will cost?

9. I really love _____, so I decided not to get a roommate.
   (being alone)

10. In my hometown, the _____ of single men of marriageable age is very
    (available group)
    small.

C. Dictation: Your teacher will read sentences with reduced forms. Listen and complete the sentences with 20 missing words. Write the full forms. (10 points)

A: Hi, Jane.

B: Hey, Terry. What's up?

A: Bad news. I think Bob _____ I are _____ break up.

B: What?!! Why?

A: Well, we had a big fight last week. I called _____ last night, and he still

   sounded _____ mad.

B: Oh?

A: I _____ if I _____ called him so soon.

B: Hmm.

A: Now I'm scared to call back. I _____ have another argument.

B: What _____ think is _____ happen?

A: Good question. What _____ do if you were me?

D. Listen to your teacher and underline the word in each sentence that is stressed for emphasis. (4 points)

  1. That's the biggest diamond ring I've ever seen.

  2. He's the man who broke my sister's heart.

  3. You're not wearing that shirt, are you?

  4. I will finish this report today, I promise!

E. Rewrite each question or statement using a different expression of doubt or uncertainty. (6 points)

  1. Should I get married or stay single?

   _____

  2. I don't think he is going to make enough money.

   _____

  3. Is Sam interested in me?

   _____

CHAPTER 4 **TEST**

A. Complete the sentences with a word or expression from the box. Change noun endings or verb forms if necessary. Not all words or expressions will be used. (10 points)

avoid	orchestra section	status symbol
chorus	prominent	threat
detract	promote	track
on hold	sold out	upcoming

1. People who have trouble falling asleep should _____ drinking coffee in the evening.

2. In modern Western societies, some possessions that could be labeled as

   _____ include large, expensive houses, expensive cars, or fine clothes.

3. Millions of dollars are spent each year to _____ the fact that if you drink alcohol, you should not drive a car.

4. When my grandmother was young, she refused to wear her glasses in public because

   she believed they _____ from her good looks.

5. The airport was closed because of a terrorist _____.

6. The entertainment section of the newspaper includes information about

   _____ movies, concerts, and musical events.

7. I phoned a theater and had to wait _____ for five minutes while a clerk got the information I had requested.

8. John Williams, who wrote the music for the *Harry Potter* movies and many others, is

   probably the most _____ composer of movie music in America.

9. By the time Steffan called the box office to get tickets to the basketball game, the

   game was _____. Next time he will call sooner.

10. My friend Brenda sings in the _____ of our city's opera company, along with 20 or 30 other singers.

B. From the box, choose a synonym for each word or expression in parentheses. Complete the sentence. Change noun endings or verb forms if necessary. (10 points)

component	mainstream	promote
emerge	make out	shrug off
genre	phenomenon	significant
lyrics	policy	sophisticated

1. The restaurant has a strict _____ : "No shoes, no service."

(rule)

2. To me, the most important _____ of a song is the melody.

(part)

3. My boss _____ the computer virus warning from the technology

(didn't worry about)

   department. Now she's waiting for her computer to be fixed!

4. I can't _____ the words to that song. He sings too softly.

(understand)

5. The emergence of rap music is the most _____ musical development

(important)

   of the last 50 years.

6. That song has a beautiful melody, but the _____ are ridiculous.

(words)

7. The music at the children's concert was not very _____, but it was

(complicated)

   loud, and the children enjoyed it.

8. Embarrassing details about the singer's personal life _____ in last

(came out)

   week's news.

9. The Beatles' music was a _____ in the world of popular music.

(unique and unusual thing)

10. In many parts of the United States, the most listened-to _____ of

(type)

    music is country music.

C. Your teacher will read the three sentences. Listen and put a mark (/) over the stressed word in each underlined phrase. (5 points)

1. The <u>recording industry</u> can't <u>crack down on</u> millions of <u>IP addresses</u>.

2. My mother told me to <u>turn off</u> the <u>DVD player</u> and get ready for my <u>piano lesson</u>, but I just <u>shrugged off</u> her request.

3. Just two years after he <u>took up</u> the guitar, Max got a job playing <u>rock music</u> at a <u>nightclub</u>.

D. Write complete sentences about each category and its subcategories. Use a different expression of classification in each sentence. (6 points)

Category	Subcategories
singers in a chorus	soprano, alto, tenor, bass
guitars	acoustic, electric

1. _____

2. _____

E. Fill in the blanks with a word or expression that signals a paraphrase. (3 points)

1. The word *timbre* is used to describe the unique aspect of an instrument's sound. _____, it is what tells our ears that a violin is a violin and a flute is a flute.

2. My tastes in music are very eclectic. _____, I enjoy many different kinds of music, from classical to rap.

3. The most prominent element of rap music is the *backbeat*, _____, the background rhythm.

F. Fill in the missing information. In the left column, fill in types of music. In the right column, fill in adjectives to explain why you like or don't like the types of music you chose. (6 points)

Type of music	Adjectives
I like _____.	1. 2. 3.
I dislike _____.	1. 2. 3.

NAME

CHAPTER 5 TEST

A. Complete the sentences with a word or expression from the box. Change noun endings or verb forms if necessary. Not all words or expressions will be used. (10 points)

account for	deal with	multitasking	qualifications
benefits	disparity	poised	range
commute	etiquette	promote	wage
courteous	fire	proper	worthwhile

1. _____ can sometimes lead to mistakes because you have too many things to think about at the same time.

2. There are three _____ for this job: three years of experience, a college degree, and fluency in English.

3. Not all companies offer _____ such as health insurance and paid vacation.

4. The government is considering raising the minimum hourly _____ from $6.75 to $7.75.

5. I don't know how to _____ impatient people.

6. Why do tobacco companies _____ cigarettes even though they are unhealthy?

7. Elias moved closer to his job in order to reduce his daily _____ by 30 minutes.

8. Nora stayed home for five years to raise her young children. This _____ the five-year gap on her résumé.

9. Even though the work was hard, it was definitely _____ because the pay was high.

10. According to the rules of _____, you should knock before you enter someone's room.

B. Write the word or expression from the box in Part A that is the <u>opposite</u> of each of the numbered words. (5 points)

1. uncomfortable, insecure	.
2. hire	
3. rude	
4. incorrect	
5. equality	

C. Your teacher will read questions and statements. Listen and draw rising ↗ or falling ↘ arrows over the underlined words to indicate the speaker's intonation. (9 points)

1. <u>Monday</u>? What's happening on <u>Monday</u>?

2. I called you <u>yesterday</u>, and I left a <u>message</u>. Did you <u>get</u> <u>it</u>?

3. Have you found a job <u>yet</u>?

4. When I was in <u>college</u>, I worked at a circus <u>part-time</u>. Can you <u>believe</u> <u>it</u>?

D. Read each situation. Ask for permission to do what is indicated. Then write a response, either giving (+) or denying (–) permission. Do not use the expressions from the example. (8 points)

EXAMPLE:
   Situation: Ask a colleague for permission to take her (his) laptop computer on a business trip.

   Q: Can I borrow your laptop?
   A: (–) I'm sorry, you can't. I need it.

1. Situation: Ask your co-worker for permission to eat lunch during your meeting.

   Q: _____

   A: (+) _____

2. Situation: Ask your boss for permission to take an extra week of vacation.

   Q: _____

   A: (–) _____

3. **Situation:** In your company cafeteria, ask the people sitting at the next table for permission to use their salt.

   Q: _____

   A: (+) _____

4. **Situation:** Ask your friend for permission to borrow his/her digital camera.

   Q: _____

   A: (−) _____

E. Write complete sentences connecting the two phrases in the items below. Use a different expression of cause or effect in each sentence. Do not use the expression in the example. *Note:* You may add words to the phrases. You may also change their order. (8 points)

   EXAMPLE:

   resign from job / not enough vacation time

   Victor resigned from his job because it didn't offer enough vacation time. _____

1. be fired / be late to work often

   _____

2. work 60 hours / get overtime pay

   _____

3. business failed / lack of clients

   _____

4. outstanding work performance / receive promotion

   _____

NAME

CHAPTER 6 TEST

A. Complete the sentence with a word or expression from the box. Change noun endings or verb forms if necessary. Not all words or expressions will be used. (10 points)

alternative	drowsiness	nutritionist
call in sick	extreme	out of it
cut down on	go from bad to worse	prescribe
deficiency	habit forming	remedy
diet	herbs	turns out

Patient: I don't know what's wrong with me. I've been feeling so _____
1
lately. I get these attacks of _____ in the middle of the day where I feel like
2
I'm going to fall asleep at my desk. And I'm thirsty all the time.

Doctor: I'd like to do some blood tests on you. From the symptoms it sounds like you

might have diabetes.

(*Later*)

Doctor: Your tests came back, and it _____ you do have diabetes.
3
Patient: You're kidding. That's awful . . . Well, what do I need to do?

Doctor: Well, first I want you to see a _____. She will give you information
4
and help you plan out a _____. She'll explain that you're going to have to
5
_____ starches, sugars, and alcohol. And I'm also going to
6
_____ some pills that will help regulate your blood sugar levels.
7
Patient: I hate taking pills. Is there any kind of _____ medicine I can take?
8
Doctor: Well, there are certain plants and _____ that you can try later, but
9
right now, I think the best _____ is a combination of exercise, eating right,
10
and medication.

B. Complete the sentences with a word or expression from the box. Change noun endings or verb forms if necessary. Not all words will be used. (9 points)

bummed out	eliminate	long term
call in sick	extreme	obese
come down with	from bad to worse	portion
deficiency	habit forming	side effect

1. **A:** What's the matter, Mara?

    B: I'm so _____. The doctor says I'm allergic to chocolate. And I

    love chocolate!

    A: What does that mean? Do you have to completely _____ chocolate

    from your diet?

    B: Yeah, if I don't want to get sick!

2. I feel weak and my throat is scratchy. I think I'm _____ a cold. I

    just can't go to work. I'm going to _____, stay home, and sleep all

    day.

3. **Customer:** Does this sleeping drug have any negative _____?

    Pharmacist: Yes, you might be a little thirsty in the morning. And be careful because it

    can be _____ if you take it every night. So follow the directions on

    the bottle and just use it occasionally, when you need it.

4. **A:** Don has been lifting weights six hours a day.

    B: That's pretty _____. He'd better be careful or he might injure

    himself.

5. I twisted my foot while I was jogging two weeks ago. Since then the pain has gone

    _____. I guess it's time to see a doctor.

6. A _____ of iron in the body can cause a condition called anemia, in

    which the blood doesn't contain enough red cells for carrying oxygen.

C. Your teacher will read complete sentences. Listen and use slashes (/) to divide them into thought groups. (6 points)

> EXAMPLE: I called the pharmacy / and asked them / to fill my prescription.

1. Lisa found out that she was allergic to cats.

2. I started to feel sick about three months ago.

3. If you feel sleepy, drink some coffee.

4. She called the doctor to change her appointment from Monday to Wednesday.

D. Respond to each of the following sentences with a different expression of sympathy. (3 points)

1. **A:** My grandmother died very suddenly last week.

   B: _____

2. **A:** I got a D on my geography exam.

   B: _____

3. **A:** Juana had a car accident. She's OK, but her car was destroyed.

   B: _____

E. Complete the short conversations. Use an expression of worry in the first blank and an expression of reassurance in the second blank. (4 points)

1. **Parent:** _____ Alice. She doesn't seem as excited about

   school as she used to be.

   Teacher: _____. She's doing fine in my class.

2. **Patient:** _____ this mole on my arm. Could it be skin cancer?

   Doctor: _____. It looks normal to me.

F. Write complete sentences about the source, using the fact given. Use a different reporting verb or phrase in each sentence. (4 points)

Source	Fact
World Health Organization	Steps must be taken to avoid an epidemic of bird flu.
A Taiwanese study	Women with higher education sleep better than uneducated women.

1. _____

_____

2. _____

_____

G. Read each pair of sentences. Write a complete sentence about the information. Use an expression of similarity or difference. (4 points)

1. Similarity

Meditation can lower cholesterol levels.	Exercise can lower cholesterol levels.

_____

_____

2. Difference

Animal protein raises cholesterol because it is also high in fat.
Plant proteins such as soy have less fat and do not raise cholesterol.

_____

_____

NAME _____

CHAPTER **7** **TEST**

A. Complete the sentences with a word or expression from the box. Change noun endings or verb forms if necessary. (10 points)

cope with	marked down	promotional
cost an arm and a leg	on sale	rip-off
good deal	pay through the nose	surcharge
ideology		

1. If you change the date of your airline ticket, you might have to pay a

   _____.

2. Linda usually buys her clothes at the end of the season because then the prices are

   _____ by 50 percent or more.

3. I decided to stop driving my car to work because nowadays gasoline and parking

   _____. By taking the bus I can save more than $100 a month.

4. The movie was really terrible. I can't believe I paid $11 for the ticket. What a

   _____!

5. I found an English teacher who will teach me for free in exchange for teaching him

   my language. Don't you think that's a _____?

6. Taka hates to shop during the holiday season because it's hard for him to

   _____ crowds.

7. You'll _____ if you buy food at this market; the prices at the

   market across the street are much lower.

8. We were able to get cheap tickets to Mexico City because our favorite airline just

   started flying there, and the company was offering a special

   _____ fare.

9. These books usually cost $25, but I bought them _____ for $12.

10. Communism is a political _____ that believes in government-

    owned businesses and does not believe in private property.

B. For each word or expression in parentheses, choose a synonym or definition from the box and complete the sentence. Change noun endings or verb forms if necessary. Not all words or expressions will be used. (10 points)

against my will	coincidence	cost a fortune	quote
as long as	competitive	countless	surcharge
ban	controversial	headquarters	valid
bargain	cope with	plagued with doubt	

1. Microsoft has offices around the world, but their _____ is in Seattle,
(main office)
Washington.

2. Many universities have _____ the sale of cigarettes on campus.
(forbidden)

3. The sale of real fur coats has become a _____ topic because so many
(debated)
people oppose it.

4. Some wedding dresses_____, but I only paid $100 for mine
(are extremely expensive)
because I got it on sale.

5. This car salesperson _____ me a much higher price than the other
(told)
salesperson did.

6. You may return these shoes to the store _____ they are not
(on the condition that)
worn.

7. I bought my twin sister a beautiful sweater for her birthday and by
_____ she bought me the same one.
(chance)

8. Be sure to shop around if you want to find an airline with the most
_____ price and best service.
(reasonable)

9. My neighbor sold me his one-year-old Nikon camera for $50 because he decided to
get a new one; that's a _____ , don't you think?
(an excellent buy)

10. The spa gave me a gift certificate that is _____ only until September 1.
(usable)

C. Circle the expression that best completes each sentence below. (4 points)

Clerk: Hi. How can I help you?

Customer: I'd like to return this because ———— (it's defective / it's marked down / it's
    1
on sale).

Clerk: Hmm. I can't give you a refund, but you can exchange it if you like. Would you

like to ———— (shop around / pay a surcharge / give me a break)?
     2

Customer: I can't get a refund? ———— (What a good deal! / What a rip-off! / What a
                  3
steal!)

Clerk: I'm sorry. It's store policy. ———— (I'm plagued with doubt. / My hands are
                     4
tied. / It's against my will.)

D. Write a complete sentence about each topic below. Use a different "pro" or "con"
    expression in each item. Do not use the expression in the example. (6 points)

EXAMPLE:

eating meat

(con) *Many members of my family are opponents of eating meat.*

1. violence in television shows for children.

   (con) _____

2. free medical care for all citizens

   (pro) _____

3. wearing real fur

   (con) _____

E. Your teacher will read the sentences below. Listen and underline the *t* or *tt* whenever
    it makes the /d/ sound. (5 points)

1. Butter can be fattening.

2. I can't get it to open.

3. She started shopping in the city.

4. Peter will wait for me until eight o'clock.

F. Your teacher will read sentences with reduced forms. Listen and write the missing words in the blanks. (5 points)

1. Can you _____ a discount on this shirt?

2. _____ find a better price?

3. _____ return this jacket and get a different one?

4. _____ meet me at the mall?

CHAPTER **8** **TEST**

A. Complete the sentences with a word or expression from the box. Change noun endings or verb forms if necessary. Not all words or expressions will be used. (5 points)

be frank	make that up	swear
a bunch of baloney	mean it	take my word for it

Father: Luke, were you at school yesterday?

Son: Yeah, dad.

Father: Are you sure?

Son: Yeah, I _____.

               1

Father: I think that's _____. Your teacher called and asked

                  2

where you were.

Son: Uh, well, I was at school, but I didn't go to class because I had a terrible stomachache. Really. If you don't want to _____, call

             3

the school nurse.

Father: Well, son, I'll _____ with you: I already called the school nurse.

             4

She said you weren't there either. I think you _____.

                     5

Son: OK, you're right. I skipped class and went to a movie. I'm really sorry, Dad.

B. Complete the sentences with a word or expression from the box. Change noun endings or verb forms if necessary. Not all words or expressions will be used. (10 points)

claim	donate	short term	turn in
determine	ethical	straight-A	versus
dilemma	loyalty	tempted	

1. The final exam grade counts for 60 percent of the final grade, so his grade on the final exam will _____ his grade in the course.

2. Would you like to _____ $100 to cancer research?

3. I don't feel any _____ to a political party. I just vote for the candidate whose ideas I like most, regardless of the party the person belongs to.

4. The police found your stolen car. You can go and _____ it at the police station.

5. Parents need to teach their children the difference between right and wrong so that children can make _____ decisions when they grow up.

6. Andrea was _____ to keep the gold watch she found, but didn't; she turned it in to the lost and found department.

7. The owner of the lost watch was grateful that Andrea_____ it _____ to the police instead of keeping it.

8. I have a huge _____: Should I go to a famous but expensive university and borrow money for the tuition, or should I go to a smaller, less famous, but more affordable college?

9. Andrew was a _____ student in high school, but his grades were just so-so in college.

10. You must consider the benefits of telling the truth to your friend _____ the pain of hurting her feelings.

C. Write the word or expression from the box that is the <u>opposite</u> of each of the numbered words below. (7 points)

build yourself up	drop off	be entitled to	make public
definitely	encourage	face (*verb*)	reward

1. maybe	
2. pick up (a person in a car)	
3. keep secret	
4. punishment	
5. hide (from a problem)	
6. have no right to (something)	
7. be shy, modest (about oneself)	

D. Find and correct an error in each expression of disbelief below. (5 points)

1. Give me the break.

2. You're putting me out.

3. I don't bring it.

4. Come out.

5. You're pulling my arm.

E. Explain the scenarios. Use a different expression each time to signal an imaginary situation. Do not use the expression in the example. (4 points)

EXAMPLE:

a friend asks to copy an old essay of yours

What if a friend asked to copy an old essay of yours?

1. you find a diamond ring in a public bathroom

_____.

2. a teacher grades you unfairly

_____.

F. Your teacher will read sentences with phrasal verbs. Listen and put a mark (✓) over the stressed words in the phrasal verbs. (4 points)

1. I thought it over and decided to tell her the truth.

2. I need to drop off my overdue library book.

3. I can turn it in for you.

4. The police have the information, but they can't give it out.

G. Your teacher will read questions and statements. Listen and circle the words you hear. (5 points)

1. Would *you / she* cheat on a test if nobody saw you?

2. She *wouldn't / would* be here without your help.

3. When *would / wouldn't* you be able to come?

4. *Wouldn't / Would* you like to know what the future brings?

5. Where would *she / you* go without a car?

SCRIPTS FOR CHAPTER TESTS

Chapter Test 1, Part D

NOTE TO TEACHER: Please read items with natural speed and intonation. Be sure to enunciate the stressed words (underlined or circled) slightly louder, more clearly, and at a higher pitch than unstressed words, but do not exaggerate them.

EXAMPLE:

I'm sorry, but I can't remember your name.

1. My brother is two years younger than I am.

2. The weather is awful today. I wish I could stay home.

3. Don't sit on the chair by the window. It's been broken since last Sunday.

4. Why are you leaving so early?

5. Ming couldn't speak English until he was 13 years old.

Chapter Test 2, Part D

NOTE TO TEACHER: Be sure to link sounds where indicted by arcs.

EXAMPLE:

He's afraid to fly, so he travels by train or by bus.

1. The thing I can't stand about traveling is the small airplane seats. It's impossible to get comfortable.

2. The security officer told me to take all my things out of the suitcase.

3. Our plane couldn't land in London because of the thick fog and heavy rain.

Chapter Test 3, Part C

NOTE TO TEACHER: Make sure to read the sentences with reduced pronunciation, as indicated below.

A: Hi, Jane.

B: Hey, Terry. What's up?

A: Bad news. I think Bob 'n' I are prob'ly gonna break up.

B: What?! Why?

A: Well, we had a big fight last week. I called 'im last night, and he still sounded kinda mad.

B: Oh?

A: I dunno if I should'uv called him so soon.

B: Hmm.

A: Now I'm scared to call back. I don' wanna have another argument.

B: What d'ya think is gonna happen?

A: Good question. What wouldjoo do if you were me?

Chapter Test 3, Part D

NOTE TO TEACHER: Read the capitalized words higher, louder, and more clearly than the other words in the sentence.

1. That's the biggest diamond ring I've EVER seen.
2. HE'S the man who broke my sister's heart.
3. You're not wearing THAT shirt, are you?
4. I WILL finish this report today, I promise!

Chapter Test 4, Part C

NOTE TO TEACHER: Read items with natural speed and intonation. Be sure to stress (but do not exaggerate) the underlined words or word parts.

1. The <u>recording</u> industry can't crack <u>down</u> on millions of <u>IP</u> addresses.
2. My mother told me to turn <u>off</u> the <u>DVD</u> player and get ready for my <u>piano</u> lesson, but I just shrugged <u>off</u> her request.
3. Just two years after he took <u>up</u> the guitar, Max got a job playing <u>rock</u> music at a <u>night</u>club.

Chapter Test 5, Part C

NOTE TO TEACHER: Read the sentences with clear but natural rising and falling intonation, as indicated.

1. Monday? ↗ What's happening on Monday? ↘
2. I called you yesterday, ↘ and I left a message. ↘ Did you get it? ↗
3. Have you found a job yet? ↗
4. When I was in college, ↗ I worked at a circus part-time. ↘ Can you believe it? ↗

Chapter Test 6, Part C

NOTE TO TEACHER: Read at natural speed. Be sure to insert pauses naturally between thought groups as indicated by slashes.

EXAMPLE:
I called the pharmacy / and asked them / to fill my prescription.

1. Lisa found out / that she was allergic / to cats.

2. I started to feel sick / about three months ago.

3. If you feel sleepy, / drink some coffee.

4. She called the doctor / to change her appointment / from Monday to Wednesday.

Chapter Test 7, Part E

NOTE TO TEACHER: Read the sentences as written.

1. Budder can be fattening.

2. I can't ged it to open.

3. She starded shopping in the cidy.

4. Peder will wait for me until eight o'clock.

Chapter Test 7, Part F

NOTE TO TEACHER: Pronounce the sentences with natural stress and intonation. Pronounce the reduced forms as they are written below.

1. Kin ya gimme a discount on this shirt?

2. Couldncha find a better price?

3. Didja wanna return this jacket 'n' get a different one?

4. Wouldja meet me at the mall?

Chapter Test 8, Part F

NOTE TO TEACHER: Read naturally. Be sure to stress the underlined words but do not exaggerate.

1. I thought it <u>over</u> and decided to tell her the truth.

2. I need to drop <u>off</u> my overdue library book.

3. I can turn it <u>in</u> for you.

4. The police have the information, but they can't give it <u>out</u>.

Chapter Test 8, Part G

NOTE TO TEACHER: Read naturally. Use reductions as indicated in parentheses.

1. Would you cheat on a test if nobody saw you? (Would-ja . . .)

2. She wouldn't be here without your help. (She would-n' be here . . .)

3. When would you be able to come? (When would-ja . . .)

4. Wouldn't you like to know what the future brings? (Wouldn'cha like . . .)

5. Where would she go without a car? (Where would she . . .—no reduction here)

ANSWER KEY FOR CHAPTER TESTS

CHAPTER 1

A. 10 points (1 point each)

1. make sense
2. differentiate
3. am sick of / can't stand
4. reputation
5. tend to
6. can't stand / am sick of
7. hassle
8. Unless
9. unconventional
10. explicit

B. 10 points (1 point each)

1. loosen up
2. in authority
3. likely
4. estimate
5. study
6. linguist
7. title
8. reaction
9. prospective
10. tendency

C. 6 points (2 points each)

(*Answers will vary.*) *For example:*

My family name is Lightfoot because one of my ancestors could run very fast.
My name is Andrew, but most people call me Andy.
There are six people in my immediate family.
I don't have a middle name.
If I have a son some day, I want to name him Joshua.
I am named for my grandmother.
My father's name is Richard, and his nickname is Rich.

D. 10 points (1 point per word)

1. brother, two
2. weather, home
3. Don't, broken
4. Why, leaving
5. couldn't, old

E. 4 points (1 point each)

1. All right, Ms. Hansen.
2. Yes sir, right away.
3. Hello, Mrs. Baker.
4. Hi, Professor Smith.

CHAPTER 2

A. 5 points (1 point per blank)

1. pay through the nose
2. deadline
3. outbreak
4. at random
5. ended up

B. 5 points (1 point each)

1. panic-stricken
2. hazardous
3. purchase
4. show up
5. messed up

C. 5 points (1 point each)

1. guidelines
2. ripped off
3. leads to
4. lack of
5. rate

D. 3 points (1 point for each linking error)

1. get comfortable
2. told me
3. heavy rain

E. 6 points (3 points for each blank)

(*Answers will vary.*)

1. All the noise and people drinking <u>annoy me</u>.
2. <u>It drives me crazy</u> when Professor Baker gives us 300 pages to read in one week.
3. <u>It bugs me</u> when people do that.

F. 6 points (3 points for each correct use of an expression of advice)

(*Answers will vary.*)

1. I recommend visiting some websites about Japan before your trip.
2. You should ask a neighbor to feed your cat.
3. You'd better take some light clothes and some sun screen, just in case.

G. 4 points (2 points each)

(*Answers will vary.*)

1. Slang can be defined as nonstandard or informal language . . .
2. Sociology refers to the study of . . .

H. 6 points (3 points each)

(*Answers will vary.*)

1. My pet peeve is narrow airplane seats.
2. A phobia is an intense, irrational fear of something or of a situation.
3. Therapy is the treatment of illness over a long period of time, without medicine.

CHAPTER 3

A. 10 points (1 point each)

1. matched up
2. assumed
3. on the basis of
4. As far as
5. passionate
6. fell head over heels in love
7. committed
8. settle down
9. wonders about
10. pursue

B. 10 points (1 point each)

1. stay out of it
2. Chances are
3. keep in mind
4. drives
5. fulfilled
6. left out
7. profiles
8. ballpark figure
9. solitude
10. pool

C. 10 points (Each boldface word is 1/2 point)

A: Hi, Jane.
B: Hey, Terry. What's up?
A: Bad news. I think Bob **and** I are **probably going to** break up.
B: What?! Why?
A: Well, we had a big fight last week. I called **him** last night, and he still sounded **kind of** mad.
B: Oh?
A: I **don't know** if I **should have** called him so soon.
B: Hmm.

A: Now I'm scared to call back. I **don't want to** have another argument.

B: What **do you** think is **going to** happen?

A: Good question. What **would you** do if you were me?

D. 4 points (1 point each)

1. That's the biggest diamond ring I've <u>ever</u> seen.
2. <u>He's</u> the man who broke my sister's heart.
3. You're not wearing <u>that</u> shirt, are you?
4. I <u>will</u> finish this report today, I promise!

E. 6 points (2 points each)

(*Answers will vary.*)

1. I'm not sure if I should get married or stay single.
2. I doubt if he is going to make enough money.
3. I wonder if Sam is interested in me.

CHAPTER 4

A. 10 points (1 point each)

1. avoid
2. status symbols
3. promote
4. detracted
5. threat
6. upcoming
7. on hold
8. prominent
9. sold out
10. chorus

B. 10 points (1 point each)

1. policy
2. component
3. shrugged off
4. make out

5. significant
6. lyrics
7. sophisticated
8. emerged
9. phenomenon
10. genre

C. 5 points (1/2 point for each stressed word)

1. recording, down, IP
2. off, DVD, piano, off
3. up, rock, night

D. 6 points (3 points each)

(*Answers will vary.*)

1. The singers in a chorus can be divided into four categories (groups): soprano, alto, tenor, and bass.
2. There are two types of guitars: acoustic and electric.

E. 3 points (1 point each)

(*Answers will vary.*)

1. <u>To put it another way</u>, it is what tells our ears that a violin is a violin and a flute is a flute.
2. <u>I mean</u>, I enjoy many different kinds of music, from classical to rap.
3. <u>in other words</u>, the background rhythm.

F. 6 points (1 point for each adjective)

(*Answers will vary.*)

CHAPTER 5

A. 10 points (1 point each)

1. Multitasking
2. qualifications
3. benefits

4. wage
5. deal with
6. promote
7. commute
8. accounts for
9. worthwhile
10. etiquette

B. 5 points (1 point each)

1. poised
2. fire
3. courteous
4. proper
5. disparity

C. 9 points (1 point each)

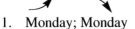

1. Monday; Monday

2. yesterday; message; get it

3. yet

4. college; part-time; believe it

D. 8 points (2 points each)

(*Answers will vary.*)

1. **Q:** Do you mind if I eat lunch during our meeting?
   A: No, not at all.
2. **Q:** Is it OK if I take an extra week of vacation?
   A: I'm afraid that's not possible.
3. **Q:** Could I use your salt?
   A: Sure.
4. **Q:** Would it be possible for me to borrow your digital camera?
   A: I'd rather you didn't.

E. 8 points (2 points each)

(*Answers will vary.*)

1. You'll be fired if you're late to work often.
2. John worked 60 hours last week. As a result, he got overtime pay.
3. The business failed due to a lack of clients.
4. Because of her outstanding work performance, Mary received a promotion.

CHAPTER 6

A. 10 points (1 point each)

1. out of it
2. drowsiness
3. turns out
4. nutritionist
5. diet
6. cut down on
7. prescribe
8. alternative
9. herbs
10. remedy

B. 9 points (1 point each)

1. bummed out
2. eliminate
3. coming down with
4. call in sick
5. side effects
6. habit forming
7. extreme
8. from bad to worse
9. deficiency

C. 6 points (1 point for each slash [/])

1. Lisa found out / that she was allergic / to cats.
2. I started to feel sick / about three months ago.

3. If you feel sleepy, / drink some coffee.
4. She called the doctor / to change her appointment / from Monday to Wednesday.

D. 3 points (1 point for each correct expression of sympathy)

(*Answers will vary.*)

1. I'm so sorry to hear that.
   My condolences.
2. What a bummer.
   That's too bad.
3. That's awful / horrible / terrible.

E. 4 points (1 point for each blank)

(*Answers will vary.*)

1. <u>I'm concerned about</u> Alice.
   <u>There's no need to worry</u>.
2. <u>I'm worried about</u> this mole on my arm.
   <u>Don't panic</u>.

F. 4 points (2 points each)

(*Answers will vary.*)

1. According to the World Health Organization, steps must be taken to avoid an epidemic of bird flu.
2. A Taiwanese study says that women with higher education sleep better than uneducated women.

G. 4 points (2 points each)

(*Answers will vary.*)

1. Both meditation and exercise can lower cholesterol levels.
2. In contrast to animal protein, plant proteins have less fat and don't raise cholesterol.

CHAPTER 7

A. 10 points (1 point each)

1. surcharge
2. marked down
3. cost an arm and a leg
4. rip-off
5. good deal
6. cope with
7. pay through the nose
8. promotional
9. on sale
10. ideology

B. 10 points (1 point each)

1. headquarters
2. banned
3. controversial
4. cost a fortune
5. quoted
6. as long as
7. coincidence
8. competitive
9. bargain
10. valid

C. 4 points (1 point each)

1. it's defective
2. shop around
3. What a rip-off!
4. My hands are tied.

D. 6 points (2 points each)

(*Answers will vary.*)

1. I am opposed to (against) violence in television shows for children.
2. I support free medical care for all citizens.
3. I am opposed to wearing real fur.

E. 5 points (1 point each)

1. Butter can be fattening.
2. I can't get it to open.
3. She started shopping in the city.
4. Peter will wait for me until
   eight o' clock.

F. 5 points (1/2 point for each word)

1. Can you give me a discount on this shirt?
2. Couldn't you find a better price?
3. Did you want to return this jacket and get a different one?
4. Would you meet me at the mall?

CHAPTER 8

A. 5 points (1 point each)

1. swear
2. a bunch of baloney
3. take my word for it
4. be frank
5. are making that up / made that up

B. 10 points (1 point each)

1. determine
2. donate
3. loyalty
4. claim
5. ethical
6. tempted
7. turned; in
8. dilemma
9. straight-A
10. versus

C. 7 points (1 point each)

1. definitely
2. drop off

3. make public
4. reward
5. face
6. be entitled to
7. build yourself up

D. 5 points (1 point for each error)

1. Give me *a* break.
2. You're putting me *on*.
3. I don't *buy* it.
4. Come *on*.
5. You're pulling my *leg*.

E. 4 points (2 points each)

(Answers will vary.)

1. Suppose you found a diamond ring in a public bathroom.
2. Let's say your teacher graded you unfairly.

F. 4 points (1 point each)

1. over
2. off
3. in
4. out

G. 5 points (1 point each)

1. you
2. wouldn't
3. would
4. Wouldn't
5. she